BTEC Level 2 First Study Skills Guide in Construction

Welcome to your Study Skills Guide! You can make it your own – start by adding your personal and course details below...

Learner's name: *Mubasir Tariq*

BTEC course title: _____

Date started: _____

Mandatory units:

_____

_____

_____

Optional units:

_____

_____

_____

Centre name: _____

Centre address: _____

_____

_____

Tutor's name: _____

Published by Pearson Education Limited, a company incorporated in England and Wales, having its registered office at Edinburgh Gate, Harlow, Essex, CM20 2JE. Registered company number: 872828

Edexcel is a registered trademark of Edexcel Limited

Text © Pearson Education Limited 2010

First published 2010

13 12 11
10 9 8 7 6 5 4 3

British Library Cataloguing in Publication Data
A catalogue record for this book is available from the British Library

ISBN 978 1 84690 576 6

Typeset and edited by Ken Vail Graphic Design
Cover design by Visual Philosophy, created by eMC Design
Cover photo/illustration © Alamy: Blend Images
Printed in Slovakia by Neografia

Acknowledgements
The publisher would like to thank the following for their kind permission to reproduce their photographs:

Alamy Images: Ace Stock Limited 55, Jacky Chapman, Janine Wiedel Photolibrary 14; **Corbis**: 62, Comstock 5; **iStockphoto**: Lisa F. Young 38; **Pearson Education Ltd**: Steve Shott 24, Ian Wedgewood 35; **Photolibrary.com**: Javier Larrea / age fotostock 42; **TopFoto**: John Powell 20

Cover images: *Front:* **Alamy Images**: Blend Images

All other images © Pearson Education

Every effort has been made to trace the copyright holders and we apologise in advance for any unintentional omissions. We would be pleased to insert the appropriate acknowledgement in any subsequent edition of this publication.

Websites
Go to www.pearsonhotlinks.co.uk to gain access to the relevant website links and information on how they can aid your studies. When you access the site, search for either the title BTEC Level 2 First Study Skills Guide in Construction or ISBN 9781846905766.

Disclaimer
This material has been published on behalf of Edexcel and offers high-quality support for the delivery of Edexcel qualifications.
This does not mean that the material is essential to achieve any Edexcel qualification, nor does it mean that it is the only suitable material available to support any Edexcel qualification. Edexcel material will not be used verbatim in setting any Edexcel examination or assessment. Any resource lists produced by Edexcel shall include this and other appropriate resources. Copies of official specifications for all Edexcel qualifications may be found on the Edexcel website: www.edexcel.com

Contents

Popular progression pathways

General qualification	Vocationally related qualification	Applied qualification
Undergraduate Degree	BTEC Higher National	Foundation Degree
GCE AS and A level	BTEC National	Advanced Diploma
GCSE	BTEC First	Higher (L2) and Foundation (L1) Diplomas

Your BTEC First course
Early days

Every year many new learners start BTEC Level 2 First courses, enjoy the challenge and successfully achieve their award. Some do this the easy way; others make it harder for themselves.

Everyone will have different feelings when they start their course.

Case study: Thinking positively

Ryan is still at school and has chosen the BTEC First in Construction as one of his Year 10 options. The course will be delivered, one day a week, at a local college. Learners will have to travel there independently.

The college is a huge establishment with a large number of learners enrolled on various courses, and so is quite daunting. Ryan is nervous about his first day. However, tutors from the college have visited the school to discuss the course, and Ryan knows what to expect. He also visited the college to have a look around before deciding to choose the BTEC First.

The first day, a course induction, goes well. The course units are explained, along with the methods of assessment. Learners go on a tour of the college and, at lunchtime, Ryan meets some of his friends who are on a different course. He settles in well and his previous worries disappear.

The BTEC First in Construction seems an exciting and challenging start to a career in construction. Ryan thinks that he will enjoy it because he can take practical units, as well as learning about the theoretical side of construction.

About your course

What do you know already?

If someone asks you about your course, could you give a short, accurate description? If you can, you have a good understanding of what your course is about. This has several benefits.

Four benefits of understanding your course

1 You will be better prepared and organised.

2 You can make links between the course and the world around you.

3 You can check how your personal interests and hobbies relate to the course.

4 You will be alert to information that relates to topics you are studying, whether it's from conversations with family and friends, watching television or at a part-time job.

Read any information you have been given by your centre. You can also check the Edexcel website for further details – go to www.edexcel.com.

Interest/hobby	How this relates to my studies

What else do you need to know?

Five facts you should find out about your course

1. The type of BTEC qualification you are studying.
2. How many credits your qualification is worth.
3. The number of core units you will study and what they cover.
4. How many credits the mandatory units are worth.
5. The number of specialist units you need to study in total and the options available in your centre.

Case study: What will I study?

Rachael, who is at school, has started her BTEC First in Construction. She finds the BTEC First course structure confusing compared to the GCSE programmes she is used to, particularly in terms of the hours and credits for each unit.

Rachael's tutor has outlined the units that the class is going to study over the coming year. For the BTEC First Certificate, Rachael has to complete six units. She will take the course on one day each week, three units per year, over two years. For more information, Rachael's tutor suggests that she visits the Edexcel website and reads this Study Guide which she was given at the beginning of the course.

The website will provide Rachael with all the information that she needs to understand the structure of the course, the combination of the units, their content and the methods of assessment. She can also download the full course specification. This will make her confident in the approach she is taking with her studies. If you wish to visit the Edexcel website to find out more about your course go to www.edexcel.com and search for construction. Click on the link for this case study.

Rachael enjoys drawing as a hobby. She is very good at it and has entered some of her work into local art competitions. Rachael's tutor sees her potential and thinks she could apply her flair for drawing to design work. He feels that architecture or interior design might be great careers for her. He suggests that she uses the internet to research job opportunities, giving her a goal to aim for.

BTEC FACT

BTEC First Certificate = 15 credits

BTEC First Extended Certificate = 30 credits

BTEC First Diploma = 60 credits

Generally, the more credits there are, the longer it takes to study for the qualification.

TRY THIS

Find out which optional units your centre offers. To check the topics covered in each unit go to www.edexcel.com and search for your qualification.

TOP TIP

If you have a choice of optional units in your centre and are struggling to decide, talk through your ideas with your tutor.

Activity: How well do you know your course?

Complete this activity to check that you know the main facts. Compare your answers with a friend. You should have similar answers except where you make personal choices, such as about optional units. Your tutor can help you complete number 9.

1 The correct title of the BTEC award I am studying is:

_____

_____

2 The length of time it will take me to complete my award is:

_____

_____

3 The number of mandatory units I have to study is:

_____

_____

4 The titles of my mandatory units, and their credit values, are:

_____

_____

_____

_____

_____

_____

_____

_____

_____

_____

5 The main topics I will learn in each mandatory unit include:

Mandatory unit	Main topics

6 The number of credits I need to achieve by studying optional units is:

7 The titles of my optional units, and their credit values, are:

8 The main topics I will learn in each optional unit include:

Optional unit	Main topics

9 Other important aspects of my course are:

10 After I have achieved my BTEC First, my options include:

Introduction to the construction sector

The construction industry is a vast and wide-ranging sector encompassing all aspects of construction work in the UK. The UK construction industry, at its peak, employs approximately 2 million people in a variety of roles, carrying out many different activities and services. The industry turns over approximately £100 billion per year, accounting for 10% of the UK's Gross Domestic Product (GDP). This means that the products made and services carried out by the construction industry contribute up to 10% of the UK's total market value each year.

The sector includes construction, civil engineering and building maintenance; employment is provided by many different types of organisation. The sector provides services in the form of architectural design, structural engineering, building services design and many different specialist consultancy and subcontractor or supplier activities.

We live, work and play within a built environment and could not do this without the buildings and other structures that provide shelter, keep us warm in winter, allow light in and provide safety and security. The architectural heritage of the UK is the envy of many visitors, who admire everything from our historical buildings to the modern constructions associated with the London 2012 Olympic Games.

There is a wide range of opportunities within the industry and there are many prospects for progressing from any starting level. The trained on-site operative and school leaver both have opportunities through education, training and experience to progress along a chosen career pathway. There are numerous professional roles within construction – such as architect, quantity surveyor, structural and civil engineer, building services engineer and construction manager – dealing with design, finance, structural design, mechanical and electrical installations and site management. All of these roles require a sound grounding in the basic Level 2 qualifications, as well as further training.

After completing a BTEC Level 2 First in Construction you can progress to a BTEC Level 3 National which allows access to Higher Education and University. Once working in your chosen career, you could join a professional association such as RIBA, ICE, RICS, CIBCIE and the CIOB. Look up these abbreviations to see what they stand for. Each professional association has a website with an education section, so you can see what is required in the long term when joining such an association.

To a young person, the industry may seem a massive operation. On your BTEC First course, take time to learn about the different roles, trades and professions before deciding which branch you want to specialise in. The right information and guidance is essential for you to succeed in the future. Learn as much as you can; well-informed students make wise career choices.

Case study: Introduction to your sector

Simon is currently studying in Year 9 at school and has been asked to consider his options for Years 10 and 11. As well as GCSEs, he could study BTEC Firsts at school with a visiting lecturer from a local college. Simon decides to apply for the BTEC First in Construction as it is a starting qualification that will give him an all-round picture of the construction industry, what it does, what types of jobs there are and how to progress within the sector.

Simon feels this is the best way forward as he is undecided between becoming a bricklayer or a joiner. The BTEC First will give him an opportunity to investigate both trades before going to college to start a craft diploma, or trying to obtain a modern apprenticeship.

Through the information and guidance given to him, Simon believes that this is the right course to study. He can do some GCSEs alongside the BTEC First, giving him the flexibility to change direction at the end of the course if he wishes.

Simon is looking forward to starting the BTEC First in Construction. His Dad is a joiner by trade and is very supportive. He is even prepared to offer Simon a modern apprenticeship place within his business should he wish to follow this career.

TOP TIP

Having a positive 'can-do' attitude to life is very important in construction.

Skills you need for your sector

Writing skills

Assessment in the BTEC First in Construction is through assignments that can be written by hand or word processed. These are graded by tutors at pass, merit or distinction. So, you are going to have to develop skills in writing reports that include all the evidence required to meet the assessment criteria.

Your written assessments should be carefully structured:

- First, set the scene, perhaps by introducing your solution to the problem you have been set or by giving a short outline of the task you have been asked to tackle.

- The second part of your report will contain the main body of evidence to meet the criteria. You should state clearly which parts of the evidence address which grading criteria (for example P1, M2), so it is easier for the tutor to assess your work. The key to any writing is only to include material that relates to the question that has been asked; don't just add stuff in to expand the content. Remember not to cut and paste information from the internet without acknowledging its source or explaining its significance as you will receive no marks for this work.

- The last stage of assessment writing is the final summary. Try to use this section to include evidence to satisfy the merit and distinction criteria which need reflection, justification and a conclusion.

Practical skills

Many of the optional units are craft based and include:

- construction drawing
- carpentry and joinery
- brickwork
- painting and decorating
- building services techniques
- plastering and dry lining
- roofing, and wall and floor tiling.

These are all hands-on activities, but your practical skills do not have to be perfect at this stage. The BTEC First may be the first time that you have had the opportunity to practise these tasks, so you are not expected to produce work that is wholly accurate.

During these practical units, you will explore the theory and the safety aspects of each area before trying out any practical skills. An important skill is to be able to reflect on this learning process within your written observations.

You will need to keep a record of your practical work to provide evidence for assessment. This could be in the form of a series of digital photographs taken during the practical operations – always make sure that you are wearing the correct Personal Protective Equipment (PPE), even when taking photos, as this is good health and safety practice.

Witness statements from your tutor and observation records are other forms of evidence to satisfy the pass criteria. Often merit and distinction criteria will test your skill levels, especially with regard to tolerances. For example if you construct a joinery item then it must be within +/− 5mm of the stated design dimensions, so the more careful you are the higher the mark you will be awarded.

Research skills

You will need to develop your ability to seek and find relevant information to answer questions in lessons and for assessments. The internet is an obvious source of information, but there are others such as craft books, technical books, technical libraries and trade association materials.

Researching on the internet can be difficult due to the vast amount of information that is held. For example, if you Google 'brick', you get 65 million results! Therefore, you are going to have to use advanced search techniques to narrow your search for relevant information.

In your assignments, always acknowledge the sources of your information in a bibliography section; write down details of the websites, books and articles you have used.

The information you use should be at the right level for your course. For example, using a university website to research types of brick might give information that is too complex for a BTEC First learner. The key is to make your writing simple and concise, don't simply cut and paste, but rework material into your own words.

Presentation skills

Your tutor may ask small groups of learners to make short presentations to the rest of the BTEC First class. This is nothing to worry about – without realising you may already have delivered verbal material to an audience, for example shouting at a football match!

- Consider using Microsoft PowerPoint or similar software to deliver professional-looking presentations.

- Make sure that at least one person in the group knows how to use the software you have chosen.

- It is helpful to divide up the work for the presentation so that each group member is given a specific task. The team leader can work with the rest of the group to pull all the material back together into a presentable format.

- When making slides, remember not to put too much information on each one and to make the text large enough to read from a distance. Use pictures and photographs to illustrate points.

Verbal communication skills

You will need to speak at some point during your course, even if just to ask or answer a question in class! If you don't know something, always ask the tutor to clarify – it's best to check, rather than make a guess and get it wrong.

- Don't mumble. Speak clearly to get your point over to the audience.

- Speaking has to be balanced with listening; to be a good speaker, you must be a good listener. Take time to hear responses and digest these before answering. Good listening is a skill that will develop over time.

- Remember, it is rude to talk over someone who has already started talking. Wait for an appropriate moment to answer or interject a comment.

- Soon you will master the art of verbal communication!

Your BTEC course will help you develop all-round skills, like communication.

Drawing skills

One of the units within BTEC First in Construction is a construction drawing unit. You will learn technical skills using a drawing board and various drawing instruments.

Technical drawing involves the use of a t-square or sliding ruler and set squares which allow you to draw pre-determined angles. Practice makes perfect! Don't be concerned if you find this skill difficult initially; you will soon master the techniques required.

Producing accurate construction drawings often involves the use of scaled diagrams. You will need to obtain a scale rule and learn how to use scales. By using scaled drawings you will be able to reduce a large building down to a manageable size on paper.

Time management skills

You should devote some time at home to work on your assignments. To make the best use of your study time, you will need to develop a work plan and stick to it! Be realistic; structure your work plan so you can study quietly for a while and have a reward when you finish. For example, an hour's work equals half an hour of football or watching television.

Taking time to complete work at home will give you the opportunity to aim for higher grades and may make you more confident in your skills. Always try to do your best and produce quality work.

Remember to back up your work onto a memory stick or disc so you don't lose it, and also so you that you can easily transport the work from your centre to home, and vice versa.

TOP TIP

Keep your work area tidy and make sure that you have washed and dried your hands. Pencil lines smudge easily and dirty finger marks transfer readily onto paper.

More about BTEC First

What is different about a BTEC First?

How you learn

Expect to be 'hands-on'. BTEC Firsts are practical and focus on the skills and knowledge needed in the workplace. You will learn new things, and learn how to apply your knowledge.

BTEC First learners are expected to take responsibility for their own learning and be keen and well-organised. You should enjoy having more freedom, while knowing you can still ask for help or support if you need it.

How you are assessed

Many BTEC First courses are completed in one year, but if you are taking GCSEs as well, you may be doing it over two years or more. You will be assessed by completing **assignments** written by your tutors. These assignments are based on **learning outcomes** set by Edexcel. Each assignment will have a deadline.

TOP TIP

Doing your best in assignments involves several skills, including managing your time so that you don't get behind. See pages 23–26 for tips on managing your time more efficiently.

BTEC FACT

On a BTEC course you achieve individual criteria at Pass, Merit or Distinction for your assignments. You will receive a Pass, Merit or Distinction **grade** for completed units and then one of these three grades for the whole course.

Case study: Why choose a BTEC First in Construction?

Saffron is thinking about taking the BTEC First in Construction. She enjoys cycling and has progressed to county level in the sport. Because of her interest, she wants to become an architect specialising in recreation and sport structures.

Saffron doesn't know whether there are any exams in the BTEC First and decides to ask her tutor. The tutor tells her that there are no exams and that assessment is normally done by written assignments. There can be small tests if the situation requires it, for example carrying out an experiment.

The tutor explains to Saffron that, in a typical unit, there are five or six pass criteria that a learner must meet in order to pass that unit. In addition, there are merit and distinction criteria; usually three merit criteria and two distinction criteria. The tutor explains that the pass criteria are roughly equivalent to a C grade at GCSE and the distinction criteria equate to an A grade.

This range of criteria gives all learners the opportunity to stretch themselves to do better. So, the harder you work, the higher the grades you achieve. This type of assessment works well for learners who become stressed during exams and underperform as a result. On a BTEC First course the pressure is continual but acceptable.

Saffron feels happy with the way that the BTEC First works and thinks that it would suit her well.

Getting the most from your BTEC

Getting the most from your BTEC involves several skills, such as using your time effectively and working well with other people. Knowing yourself is also important.

Knowing yourself

How would you describe yourself? Make some notes here.

_____

_____

_____

_____

_____

_____

_____

_____

If you described yourself to someone else, would you be able to sum up your temperament and personality, identify your strengths and weaknesses and list your skills? If not, is it because you've never thought about it or because you honestly don't have a clue?

Learning about yourself is often called self-analysis. You may have already done personality tests or careers profiles. If not, there are many available online. However, the information you gain from these profiles is useless unless you can apply it to what you are doing.

Your personality

Everyone is different. For example, some people:

- like to plan in advance; others prefer to be spontaneous
- love being part of a group; others prefer one or two close friends
- enjoy being the life and soul of the party; others prefer to sit quietly and feel uncomfortable at large social gatherings
- are imaginative and creative; others prefer to deal only with facts
- think carefully about all their options before making a decision; others follow their 'gut instincts' and often let their heart rule their head.

Case study: Gaining confidence

Kim is quiet, shy and often afraid to speak out in class. When she starts the BTEC First in Construction, she realises that everyone else is also a bit apprehensive because they have not yet settled into the programme.

Speaking freely in front of people that you don't know can be daunting, but it is not impossible. You must be positive; try not to think about looking silly or messing up the piece you are trying to communicate. Kim tries thinking positively the first time she has to speak in front of her peers. She makes the class laugh, which breaks the ice, and the whole thing becomes a lot easier. Gradually, she realises that it doesn't matter what others think.

No matter how confident they are, everyone makes mistakes. The best way to minimise the risk of messing up a presentation is to practise. Kim always practises before a presentation and is overcoming her shyness to become quite a proficient public speaker.

As your knowledge base expands through your studies, your confidence will grow, possibly to an extent that you would not have expected. After two months, Kim has learned a lot about construction and feels that she has a good knowledge base to draw on when speaking.

We are all unique; our abilities, skills, temperament and personality are very different and mean that we react to situations in different ways. Look closely at yourself to evaluate what skills you have now and which ones you would like to develop.

TRY THIS

Imagine one of your friends is describing your best features. What would they say?

Personalities in the workplace

There's a mix of personalities in most workplaces. Some people prefer to work behind the scenes, such as many IT practitioners, who like to concentrate on tasks they enjoy doing. Others love high-profile jobs, where they may often be involved in high-pressure situations, such as paramedics and television presenters. Most people fall somewhere between these two extremes.

In any job there will be some aspects that are more appealing and interesting than others. If you have a part-time job you will already know this. The same thing applies to any course you take!

Your personality and your BTEC First course

Understanding your personality means you can identify which parts of your course you are likely to find easy and which more difficult. Working out the aspects you need to develop should be positive. You can also think about how your strengths and weaknesses may affect other people.

- Natural planners find it easier to schedule work for assignments.
- Extroverts like giving presentations and working with others but may overwhelm quieter team members.
- Introverts often prefer to work alone and may be excellent at researching information.

> **BTEC FACT**
>
> All BTEC First courses enable you to develop your personal, learning and thinking skills (**PLTS**), which will help you to meet new challenges more easily. (See page 89.)

Activity: What is your personality type?

1a) Identify your own personality type, either by referring to a personality test you have done recently or by going online and doing a reliable test. Go to page 98 to find out how to access a useful website for this activity.

Print a summary of the completed test or write a brief description of the results for future reference.

b) Use this information to identify the tasks and personal characteristics that you find easy or difficult.

	Easy	Difficult
Being punctual		
Planning how to do a job		
Working neatly and accurately		
Being well organised		
Having good ideas		
Taking on new challenges		
Being observant		
Working with details		
Being patient		
Coping with criticism		
Dealing with customers		
Making decisions		
Keeping calm under stress		
Using your own initiative		

	Easy	Difficult
Researching facts carefully and accurately		
Solving problems		
Meeting deadlines		
Finding and correcting own errors		
Clearing up after yourself		
Helping other people		
Working as a member of a team		
Being sensitive to the needs of others		
Respecting other people's opinions		
Being tactful and discreet		
Being even-tempered		

2 Which thing from your 'difficult' list do you think you should work on improving first? Start by identifying the benefits you will gain. Then decide how to achieve your goal.

Your knowledge and skills

You already have a great deal of knowledge, as well as practical and personal skills gained at school, at home and at work (if you have a part-time job). Now you need to assess these to identify your strengths and weaknesses.

To do this accurately, try to identify evidence for your knowledge and skills. Obvious examples are:

- previous qualifications
- school reports
- occasions when you have demonstrated particular skills, such as communicating with customers or colleagues in a part-time job.

Part-time jobs give you knowledge and skills in a real work setting.

Activity: Check your skills

1   Score yourself from 1 to 5 for each of the skills in the table opposite.

    1 = I'm very good at this skill.

    2 = I'm good but could improve this skill.

    3 = This skill is only average and I know that I need to improve it.

    4 = I'm weak at this skill and must work hard to improve it.

    5 = I've never had the chance to develop this skill.

    Enter the score in the column headed 'Score A' and add today's date.

2   Look back at the units and topics you will be studying for your course – you entered them into the chart on pages 9–10. Use this to identify any additional skills that you know are important for your course and add them to the table. Then score yourself for these skills, too.

3   Identify the main skills you will need in order to be successful in your chosen career, and highlight them in the table.

    Go back and score yourself against each skill after three, six and nine months. That way you can monitor your progress and check where you need to take action to develop the most important skills you will need.

English and communication skills	Score A (today) Date:	Score B (after three months) Date:	Score C (after six months) Date:	Score D (after nine months) Date:
Reading and understanding different types of texts and information				
Speaking to other people face to face				
Speaking clearly on the telephone				
Listening carefully				
Writing clearly and concisely				
Presenting information in a logical order				
Summarising information				
Using correct punctuation and spelling				
Joining in a group discussion				
Expressing your own ideas and opinions appropriately				
Persuading other people to do something				
Making an oral presentation and presenting ideas clearly				

ICT skills	Score A (today) Date:	Score B (after three months) Date:	Score C (after six months) Date:	Score D (after nine months) Date:
Using ICT equipment correctly and safely				
Using a range of software				
Accurate keyboarding				
Proofreading				
Using the internet to find and select appropriate information				
Using ICT equipment to communicate and exchange information				
Producing professional documents which include tables and graphics				
Creating and interpreting spreadsheets				
Using PowerPoint				

Maths and numeracy skills	Score A (today) Date:	Score B (after three months) Date:	Score C (after six months) Date:	Score D (after nine months) Date:
Carrying out calculations (eg money, time, measurements, etc) in a work-related situation				
Estimating amounts				
Understanding and interpreting data in tables, graphs, diagrams and charts				
Comparing prices and identifying best value for money				
Solving routine and non-routine work-related numerical problems				

Case study: Skills you already have

James is not sure that he will be able to manage the work in the BTEC First in Construction. He is worried that the course will be too hard for him and that he will struggle. The local college will be delivering some of the units in partnership with James's school, so the learners have been invited to visit, meet the tutor and have a chat about the course.

As they sit around a table to have an informal discussion, James suddenly realises that everyone else feels the same way he does. The college tutor slowly explains all about the content of the course, how learners are assessed, the amount of work that is required and how long it takes to finish the full qualification.

James's tutor decides to find out what skills the group already has and so undertakes a skills audit. This is a series of questions designed to analyse an individual's strengths and weaknesses in certain areas. The audit gives the tutor and the learners an indication of what they are good at and where they can improve.

James realises, after doing the audit, that he has great report-writing skills which will help him enormously when completing his assignments. He soon forgets about his concerns as he realises that he already has lots of applicable skills, and that he can develop many more as he works through the BTEC First course.

Managing your time

Some people are brilliant at managing their time. They do everything they need to and have time left over for activities they enjoy. Other people complain that they don't know where the time goes.

Which are you? If you need help to manage your time – and most people do – you will find help here.

Why time management is important

- It means you stay in control, get less stressed and don't skip important tasks.
- Some weeks will be peaceful, others will be hectic.
- The amount of homework and assignments you have to do will vary.
- As deadlines approach, time always seems to go faster.
- Some work will need to be done quickly, maybe for the next lesson; other tasks may need to be done over several days or weeks. This needs careful planning.
- You may have several assignments or tasks to complete in a short space of time.
- You want to have a social life.

Avoiding time-wasting

We can all plan to do work, and then find our plans go wrong. There may be several reasons for this. How many of the following do *you* do?

Top time-wasting activities
1 Allowing (or encouraging) people to interrupt you.
2 Not having the information, handouts or textbook you need because you've lost them or lent them to someone else.
3 Chatting to people, making calls or sending texts when you should be working.
4 Getting distracted because you simply must keep checking out MySpace, Facebook or emails
5 Putting off jobs until they are a total nightmare, then panicking.
6 Daydreaming.
7 Making a mess of something so you have to start all over again.

Planning and getting organised

The first step in managing your time is to plan ahead and be well organised. Some people are naturally good at this. They think ahead, write down their commitments in a diary or planner, and store their notes and handouts neatly and carefully so they can find them quickly.

How good are your working habits?

Improving your planning and organisational skills

1. Use a diary or planner to schedule working times into your weekdays and weekends.

2. Have a place for everything and everything in its place.

3. Be strict with yourself when you start work. If you aren't really in the mood, set a shorter time limit and give yourself a reward when the time is up.

4. Keep a diary in which you write down exactly what work you have to do.

5. Divide up long or complex tasks into manageable chunks and put each 'chunk' in your diary with a deadline of its own.

6. Write a 'to do' list if you have several different tasks. Tick them off as you go.

7. Always allow more time than you think you need for a task.

Talking to friends can take up a lot of time.

Case study: Getting yourself organised

Time is precious; don't waste it while you are studying BTEC First in Construction. Stephen is a Year 10 student who started his course in September. It is now May and, so far, he has not managed his time very well. He has got so behind with his assessments that he needs to do lots of additional work in order to catch up.

So, how is Stephen going to catch up? He starts by discussing the problem with his tutor, who suggests that Stephen could eat his sandwiches in the classroom and use lunchtimes to catch up on his work. Stephen thinks this over and accepts his tutor's suggestion. Usually he just plays football at lunchtime, so this would be an effective use of his break.

Stephen works hard at lunchtimes for three weeks and surprises his tutor by catching up, even attempting some of the merit questions. Because of the effort that he has made, his fellow learners respect Stephen a lot more and he feels he can now hold his own on the course.

Stephen has decided he needs to plan his time more carefully so that he doesn't fall behind again. He plans a quiet period each week when he can do some work on his assignments. He knows that he has to find somewhere that he won't be disturbed and can concentrate to the best of his ability. He also makes a schedule that shows when assessments will be issued and when they have to be handed in, so he is now much more aware of his workload and can manage the deadlines.

He finds life on the course runs a lot more smoothly if he plans his time carefully.

TOP TIP

If you become distracted by social networking sites or email when you're working, set yourself a time limit of 10 minutes.

BTEC FACT

If you have serious problems that are interfering with your ability to work or to concentrate, talk to your tutor. BTEC learners who have personal difficulties can be supported in many ways to help them continue with their studies.

Activity: Managing time

1   The correct term for something you do in preference to starting a particular task is a 'displacement activity'. In the workplace this includes things like often going to the water cooler to get a drink, and constantly checking emails and so on online. People who work from home may tidy up, watch television or even cook a meal to put off starting a job.

Write down *your* top three displacement activities.

2 Today is Wednesday. Sajid has several jobs to do tonight and has started well by making a 'to do' list. He's worried that he won't get through all the things on his list and because he works on Thursday and Friday evenings that the rest will have to wait until Saturday.

a) Look through Sajid's list and decide which jobs are top priority and *must* be done tonight and which can be left until Saturday if he runs out of time.

b) Sajid is finding that his job is starting to interfere with his ability to do his assignments. What solutions can you suggest to help him?

Jobs to do

- File handouts from today's classes

- Phone Tom (left early today) to tell him the time of our presentation tomorrow has been changed to 11 am

- Research information online for next Tuesday's lesson

- Complete table from rough notes in class today

- Rewrite section of leaflet to talk about at tutorial tomorrow

- Write out class's ideas for the charity of the year, ready for course representatives meeting tomorrow lunchtime

- Redo handout Tom and I are giving out at presentation

- Plan how best to schedule assignment received today – deadline 3 weeks

- Download booklet from website ready for next Monday's class

TRY THIS

Write down your current commitments and how long they take each week. Then decide those that are top priority and those that you could postpone in a very busy week.

Getting the most from work experience

On some BTEC First courses, all learners have to do a **work placement**. On others, they are recommended but not essential, or are required only for some optional units. If you are doing one, you need to prepare for it so that you get the most out of it. The checklists in this section will help.

Before you go checklist

1. Find out about the organisation by researching online.

2. Check that you have all the information you'll need about the placement.

3. Check the route you will need to take and how long it will take you. Always allow longer on the first day.

4. Check with your tutor what clothes are suitable and make sure you look the part.

5. Check that you know any rules or guidelines you must follow.

6. Check that you know what to do if you have a serious problem during the placement, such as being too ill to go to work.

7. Talk to your tutor if you have any special personal concerns.

8. Read the unit(s) that relate to your placement carefully. Highlight points you need to remember or refer to regularly.

9. Read the assessment criteria that relate to the unit(s) and use these to make a list of the information and evidence you'll need to obtain

10. Your tutor will give you an official logbook or diary – or just use a notebook. Make notes each evening while things are fresh in your mind, and keep them safely.

While you're on work placement

Ideally, on your first day you'll be told about the company and what you'll be expected to do. You may even be allocated to one particular member of staff who will be your 'mentor'. However, not all organisations operate like this and if everyone is very busy, your **induction** may be rushed. If so, stay positive and watch other people to see what they're doing. Then offer to help where you can.

TRY THIS

You're on work experience. The placement is interesting and related to the job you want to do. However, you've been watching people most of the time and want to get more involved. Identify three jobs you think you could offer to do.

While you're there

1 Arrive with a positive attitude, knowing that you are going to do your best and get the most out of your time there.

2 Although you may be nervous at first, don't let that stop you from smiling at people, saying 'hello' and telling them your name.

3 Arrive punctually – or even early – every day. If you're delayed for any reason, phone and explain. Then get there as soon as you can.

4 If you take your mobile phone, switch it off when you arrive.

5 If you have nothing to do, offer to help someone who is busy or ask if you can watch someone who is doing a job that interests you.

6 Always remember to thank people who give you information, show you something or agree that you can observe them.

7 If you're asked to do something and don't understand what to do, ask for it to be repeated. If it's complicated, write it down.

8 If a task is difficult, start it and then check back that you are doing it correctly before you go any further.

9 Obey all company rules, such as regulations and procedures relating to health and safety and using machinery, the use of IT equipment and access to confidential information.

10 Don't rush off as fast as you can at the end of the day. Check first with your mentor or supervisor whether you can leave.

Coping with problems

Problems are rare but can happen. The most common ones are being bored because you're not given any work to do or upset because you feel someone is treating you unfairly. Normally, the best first step is to talk to your mentor at work or your supervisor. However, if you're very worried or upset, you may prefer to get in touch with your tutor instead – do it promptly.

TOP TIP

Observing people who are skilled at what they do helps you learn a lot, and may even be part of your **assignment brief.**

Getting experience of work in the construction sector

If required, your centre will coordinate a short period of work experience for you. You must make the most of this placement as it will give you valuable industrial experience. Here are some activities to help you get the most out of your time with an employer.

1 Identify which of these would be classed as a hazard on a construction site:

   a) fully enclosed electrical cable

   b) can of petrol in secure store

   c) exposed asbestos insulation

   d) MDF furniture

   e) cardboard waste in a locked skip.

2 Think about the workplace you will be attending. Identify three measures that could be taken to prevent an accident occurring to people other than employees.

   a)

   b)

   c)

Activity: Keeping a work placement logbook

Complete the following table so you have a record of your work experience.

Employer	
Address	
Mentor while at work	
Type of business	
Start date	
Finish date	
Duties	
Responsibilities	
Notes	

Activity: Reflecting on work experience

Produce a short piece of writing reflecting on your work experience. Include what went well and things that could have been better. What lessons have you learned to help you in future placements or when you enter employment?

Activity: People in the workplace

Think about someone who made a positive (or a negative) impression on you during your work placement and answer the following questions:

1 How did this person let you know what you had to do at work? Did their manner have an impact on how you performed?

2   Compare your behaviour at work and at college. Did you pick up any tips from this person on how to behave (or how not to conduct yourself) at work?

3   Did you find this person interesting or not? How can **you** make people interested in what **you** have to say?

4   At the end of your placement what should you do to make sure you remember everything that you learned? Don't forget to write a thank you letter to your employer and to include the work experience on your CV.

Case study: Making the most of a work placement

Ben has a work placement at a local builders' merchant. He really enjoys his first day. He spends a lot of time in the yard, but has to be vigilant because of the crane that operates there. There are other hazards in the yard; heavy lorries deliver building materials and hydraulic forklift trucks unload them. Due to all the moving machinery, Ben has to be very alert. He listens carefully to what he is told and follows exactly the instructions he is given.

As part of the safe systems of work, Ben has to wear a high-visibility jacket so the forklift truck drivers can see him and safety footwear so his feet are protected from injury.

As well as working in the yard, Ben also works with security staff, spends time attending to counter sales and answering the telephone sales line. This gives him a wide range of understanding and knowledge about the business.

At the end of the placement, Ben feels the experience has given him confidence and self-esteem. The manager has even mentioned the possibility of a Saturday job in the future. Ben is extremely pleased with himself; he has worked hard during this placement and it seems that he could be rewarded with potential employment in the future.

Working with other people

Everyone finds it easy to work with people they like and far harder with those they don't. On your course you'll often be expected to work as a team to do a task. This gives you practice in working with different people.

You will be expected to:

- contribute to the task
- listen to other people's views
- adapt to other people's ways of working
- take responsibility for your own contribution
- agree the best way to resolve any problems.

These are quite complex skills. It helps if you understand the benefits to be gained by working cooperatively with other people and know the best way to achieve this.

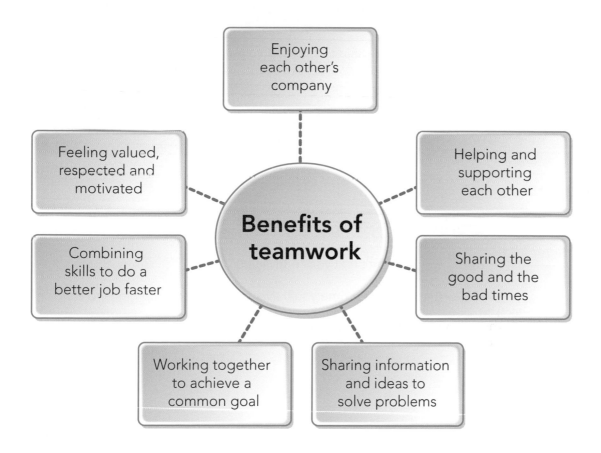

Benefits of teamwork

TOP TIP

Being a good team member means putting the group's needs before your own.

Golden rules for everyone (including the team leader!)

The secret of a successful team is that everyone works together. The role of the team leader is to make this as easy as possible by listening to people's views and coordinating everyone's efforts. A team leader is not there just to give orders.

Positive teamwork checklist

✔ Be loyal to your team, including the team leader.

✔ Be reliable and dependable at all times.

✔ Be polite. Remember to say 'please' and 'thank you'.

✔ Think before you speak.

✔ Treat everyone the same.

✔ Make allowances for individual personalities. Give people 'space' if they need it, but be ready to offer support if they ask for it.

✔ Admit mistakes and apologise if you've done something wrong – learn from it but don't dwell on it.

✔ Give praise when it's due, give help when you can and thank people who help you.

✔ Keep confidences, and any promises that you make.

TRY THIS

Work out whether you're usually passive, assertive or aggressive when you're annoyed. You've arranged to meet Sam to see a film. He arrives 20 minutes late.

Do you:

a) shrug and say nothing in case he gets upset

b) ask why he didn't text you to give you warning

c) say that it's the last time you'll ever go anywhere with him and walk off?

Which do you think would be the most effective – and why?

Case study: Teamworking in construction

Mohamed has only lived in the UK for two years and now has a basic knowledge of the English language. On work placement he finds that people are ignoring him. He thinks they probably feel slightly awkward communicating with him.

Mohamed is unsure of what to do and discusses it with his tutor on the 'phone. His tutor explains that Mohamed should try to become more proactive and assertive which will give him confidence. He suggests that Mohamed starts to ask questions about what he should be doing, so he can become more involved and better integrated into the workplace. His tutor tells him to speak slowly and clearly so staff can understand what he is trying to convey. Mohamed starts by asking his supervisor questions.

As a result his supervisor, seeing that Mohamed has started to take an interest, gives him some more important jobs to do.

Soon, Mohamed is laughing and joking with his work mates and feels that he is becoming a part of the team. The other team members are young and Mohamed feels he can relate to them. He asks them to explain the customer service level agreements as he does not know what these are. Someone explains that these agreements look at how well you perform for a customer, for example, how long it takes to serve them.

Mohammed now realises that the staff were under pressure to perform and he was just getting in the way. Now he has started to ask questions, he is learning new things and is integrating as well.

There are many benefits to be gained from working as a team.

Activity: Teamwork assessment

1 When working within a team, you must have certain skills to be effective. The following table has a list of team skills on the left-hand side. On the right-hand side, write in an example for each. The first one is completed for you.

Skill	Example
communication in the team	speak clearly and ask again if you don't understand an instruction
competitiveness	
team motivation	
team management	

2 You have just started work experience on a local construction site, working in the office to help order materials for a large project.
This involves using some skills that you have already, but that you have not applied to this context before. Below is a table with skills on the left. On the right, write how you could apply these to ordering materials.

Skill	Application
mathematics	
written communication	
verbal communication	
organising filing	
interpreting drawn information	
accuracy	

3 When you are using the telephone to communicate with other people – which you will have to do as part of a construction team – you need excellent verbal communication skills. Imagine that you are working in a busy construction-site office. List three things you should do while talking to another person on the 'phone. The first has been filled in for you.

a) Make sure they can hear you.

b)

_____

_____

_____

c)

_____

_____

_____

4 Now let's look at the team skills you could bring to a construction site or office. What skills do you have already? These could be qualities like punctuality or accuracy. Think also about the skills that you need to develop in the future for your chosen career. Use the table below to help you analyse your current and future skill needs. This will be useful when planning your progression and qualifications route.

Current team skills	Skills required in future

Getting the most from special events

BTEC First courses usually include several practical activities and special events. These enable you to find out information, develop your skills and knowledge in new situations and enjoy new experiences. They may include visits to external venues, visits from specialist speakers, and team events.

A visit to a construction site will give you a real idea of what kind of job you might like to do in the future.

Most learners enjoy the chance to do something different. You'll probably look forward to some events more than others. If you're ready to get actively involved, you'll usually gain the most benefit. It also helps to make a few preparations!

Case study: Guest speakers

The architect who designed the iconic Manchester Hilton Tower is visiting Miki's school to speak to the learners on the BTEC First course in Construction. Miki is really looking forward to it; it will be quite an honour to hear such an important person give a talk.

The tutor prepares for the guest speaker's visit by showing the learners photographs of the Manchester Hilton Tower. She asks them each to prepare three questions to raise at the end of the talk. The tutor collates the best questions and sends these to the architect in advance. Miki thinks this is a good idea as sensible questions will be asked, not silly ones, and the architect will have a chance to prepare answers.

On the day of the visit, the tutor reminds the learners to behave politely, taking time to listen and asking their questions when directed to do so. Because of the preparation work, the guest architect's visit goes so well that a work experience placement with the architectural firm is offered to the class.

After the talk, Miki reflected on what he had learned. Miki realised that the architect had a hard job convincing the city planners to build such a tall building within an underdeveloped location. He learned that if you take the lead in investing in an underdeveloped area, others follow and this can create jobs and wealth.

Special events checklist

✔ Check you understand how the event relates to your course.

✔ If a visit or trip is not something you would normally find very interesting, try to keep an open mind. You might get a surprise!

✔ Find out what you're expected to do, and any rules or guidelines you must follow, including about your clothes or appearance.

✔ Always allow enough time to arrive five minutes early, and make sure you're never late.

✔ On an external visit, make notes on what you see and hear. This is essential if you have to write about it afterwards, use your information to answer questions in an assignment or do something practical.

✔ If an external speaker is going to talk to your class, prepare a list of questions in advance. Nominate someone to thank the speaker afterwards. If you want to record the talk, it's polite to ask first.

✔ For a team event, you may be involved in planning and helping to allocate different team roles. You'll be expected to participate positively in any discussions, to talk for some (but not all) of the time, and perhaps to volunteer for some jobs yourself.

✔ Write up any notes you make as soon as you can – while you can still understand what you wrote!

TRY THIS

At the last minute, you're asked to propose a vote of thanks to a visiting speaker on behalf of your class. What would you say?

Activity: Preparing for a site visit

1 A site visit to a local construction project has been arranged for your group. This special event has involved a great deal of planning by your tutor, including obtaining parental consents and insurance cover, and doing risk assessments.

The tutor has explained that you must behave in an acceptable manner during this visit as you will be representing your centre. How will you do this? Write down three ways in which you will achieve this.

a)

b)

c)

2 You are going to interview the site manager and will need to prepare three questions to ask. Using the unit specification, prepare three questions that will extend your understanding and knowledge of construction activities.

   a)

   b)

   c)

3 One aim of your visit is to learn about keeping safe on a construction site. Identify three measures that will protect you during your visit.

   a)

   b)

   c)

Resources and research

Understanding resources

Resources are items that help you do something. The most obvious one is money! To obtain your BTEC First award, however, your resources are more widespread than just money.

Physical resources

Physical resources are things like textbooks, computers and any specialist equipment.

- Popular textbooks, laptops for home use and specialist equipment may need to be booked. Leaving it until the last minute is risky.
- You can ask for help if you don't know how to use resources properly.
- You should check what stationery and equipment you need at the start of your course and make sure you have it.
- You need to look after your resources carefully. This saves money and time spent replacing lost items.

TOP TIP

Life is a lot easier if you have all the resources you need and you take care of them. Lending important notes can hold you up (so photocopy them instead). Lending your course book may mean you can't complete work you have to do. Lending one of your assignments could get you in serious trouble!

People as resources

There are many people who can help you through your course:
- family members who help and support you
- your tutor
- friends in your group who collect handouts for you and phone you to keep you up-to-date when you're absent
- librarians and computer technicians, at your centre or your local library
- expert practitioners.

Expert practitioners

Expert practitioners have worked hard to be successful in their chosen area. They know the skills and knowledge needed to do the job properly. They can be invaluable when you're researching information (see page 44). You can also learn a lot by watching them at work, especially if you can ask them questions about what they do, what they find hard and any difficulties they've had.

Constuction experts will be a valuable source of information when researching.

TRY THIS

You may not have to make a special visit to observe an expert practitioner at work. Often television programmes (and YouTube clips) give great insights into the way a job can or should be done. See if you can find clips of someone you admire in your own vocational area by searching on YouTube or Google.

Try to observe more than one expert practitioner:
- It gives you a better picture about what they do.
- No single job will cover all aspects of work that might apply to your studies.
- You may find some experts more approachable and easy to understand than others. For example, if someone is impatient because they're busy it may be difficult to ask them questions, or if someone works very quickly you may find it hard to follow what they're doing.

If you have problems, just note what you've learned and compare it with your other observations. And there's always the chance that you're observing someone who's not very good at their job! You'll only know this for certain if you've seen what people *should* be doing.

Using resources

Resources are essential sources of information. There are many different types of resource available for you to use when completing your written assignment work. Remember that you should always acknowledge the source and put the information you have found into your own words, rather than cutting and pasting it into a document.

There are several resources available for construction students to use:

- **Libraries** – a library is normally catalogued using a reference index to enable users to find what they are looking for. Using your centre library or a local authority library, find out what the classification is for construction books on brickwork and joinery.
- **The internet** – this resource is vast; try typing the word 'construction' into a search engine to find out how many hits you get. You will probably get well over 300 million results, demonstrating the need to be selective in your approach when using the internet for research. Bear in mind that not all information is from acknowledged sources and some could be false.
- **Technical Indexes** – technical indexes and directories detailing industry standards are produced by several organisations within the Construction Sector. For example, RIBA produces a 'Product Selector' which allows you to search for construction product and service information for building design projects. The Barbour Index is also a useful source of information for those in the industry.
- **CD-ROMs** – many trade suppliers produce information on CD-ROM, for example Hepworth Drainage products.
- **Suppliers' information** – construction material suppliers often produce a variety of printed information which may be useful for your research.

Activity: Finding resources

1 In a small team, identify a supplier that produces electronic literature on **CD-ROM** and obtain a copy. Make sure that each team chooses a different supplier so a library of CD-ROMs can be built up for all to use.

2 Using the **internet** and a search engine find a manufacturer for each of the following common construction materials.

Material	Manufacturer
facing brick	
concrete	
mineral wool insulation	
plasterboard	

3 Try producing a **formal letter** requesting information from a manufacturer on a specific construction item.

Finding the information you need

The information explosion

There are lots of different ways to find out information – books, newspapers, magazines, TV, radio, CDs, DVDs, the internet. And you can exchange information with other people by texting, sending an email or phoning someone.

All this makes it much easier to obtain information. If you know what you're doing, you can probably find most of what you need sitting at a computer. But there are some dangers:

- Finding exactly what you want online takes skill. You need to know what you're doing.
- It's easy to get too much information and become overwhelmed.
- It's unlikely that everything you need will be available online.
- The information you read may be out of date.
- The information may be neither reliable nor true.

| Define what you are trying to find. (The more precise you are, the more likely you are to find what you're looking for.) | → | Know where to look for it. (Remember: the internet is not the only source of information.) | → | Recognise when you have found appropriate information. |

| Know what to do with information once you've found it. (Make sure that you understand it, interpret it correctly and record the source where you found it.) | ← | Know when to stop looking (especially if you have a deadline). |

Finding and using information effectively

Before you start

There are four things that will help you look in the right place and target your search properly.

Ask yourself ...	Because ...	Example
Exactly what do I need to find out?	It will save you time and effort.	If you need information about accidents, you need to know what type of accident and over what time period.
Why do I need this information and who is going to read it?	This puts the task into context. You need to identify the best type of information to obtain and how to get it.	If you're making a poster or leaflet for children, you'll need simple information that can be presented in a graphical format. If, however, you're giving a workplace presentation on accidents, you'll need tables and graphs to illustrate your talk.
Where can I find it?	You need to consider whether your source is trustworthy and up to date. The internet is great, but you must check that the sites you use are reliable.	To find out about accidents in the workplace you could talk to the health and safety at work officer. To find examples of accidents in your local area you could look through back copies of your local newspaper in the local library or newspaper offices.
What is my deadline?	You know how long you have to find the information and use it.	

TRY THIS

Schedule your research time by calculating backwards from the deadline date. Split the time you have 50/50 between searching for information and using it. This stops you searching for too long and getting lots of interesting material, but then not having the time to use it properly!

Your three main sources of information are libraries or learning resource centres, the internet, and other people, for example asking questions through interviews and questionnaires.

Researching in libraries

You can use the learning resource centre in your school or college, or a local public library. Public libraries usually have a large reference section with many resources available for loan, including CD-ROMs, encyclopaedias, government statistics, magazines, journals and newspapers, and databases such as Infotrac, which contains articles from newspapers and magazines over the last five years.

The librarian will show you how to find the resources you need and how to look up a specific book (or author) to check if it is available or is out on loan.

Some books and resources can only be used in the library itself, while others can be taken out on short-term or long-term loan. You need to plan how to access and use the resources that are popular or restricted.

Using your library

✔ If your centre has an intranet you might be able to check which books and CD-ROMs are available without actually visiting the library.

✔ All libraries have photocopying facilities, so take enough change with you to copy articles that you can't remove. Write down the source of any article you photocopy, ie the name and the date of the publication.

✔ Learn how to keep a reference file (or bibliography) in which you store the details of all your sources and references. A bibliography must include CDs, DVDs and other information formats, not just books and magazines.

✔ If your search is complicated, go at a quiet time when the librarian can help you.

✔ Don't get carried away if you find several books that contain the information you need. Too many can be confusing.

✔ Use the index to find information quickly by searching for key words. Scan the index using several likely alternatives.

✔ Only use books that you find easy to understand. A book is only helpful if you can retell the information in your own words.

TRY THIS

Search engines don't just find websites. On Google, the options at the top of your screen include 'images', 'news' and 'maps'. If you click on 'more' and then 'even more', you'll find other options, too. You'll usually find the most relevant information if you use the UK version of a search engine. Only search the whole web if you deliberately want to include European and American information.

Go to page 98 to find out how to see this in action.

Researching online

A good search engine such as Google will help you find useful websites. They look for sites based on the information you enter in the search box. In some cases, such as Ask.co.uk, you may get the chance to refine your choice after entering your key words or question.

Finding information on a website

Wikipedia is a popular free online encyclopaedia. It has been criticised because entries may be inaccurate as members of the public can edit the site. However, Wikipedia is trying to prevent this by organising professional editing.

If you're not sure whether something you read is correct, or if there is anything strange about it, check it against information on another site. Make sure you ask your tutor's opinion, too.

With large websites, it can be difficult to find what you need. Always read the whole screen – there may be several menus in different parts of the screen.

To help you search, many large websites have:
- their own search facility or a site map that lists site content with links to the different pages
- links to similar sites where you might find more information. Clicking a link should open a new window, so you'll still be connected to the original site.

There may be useful information and links at the top, foot or either side of a web page.

There are several other useful sites you could visit when researching online.

- **Directory sites** show websites in specific categories so you can focus your search at the start.
- **Forums** are sites, or areas of a website, where people post comments on an issue. They can be useful if you want to find out opinions on a topic. You can usually read them without registering.
- **News sites** include the BBC website as well as the sites for all the daily newspapers. Check the website of your local newspaper, too.

Printing information

- Only print information that you're sure will be useful. It's easy to print too much and find yourself drowning in paper.
- Make quick notes on your print-outs so that you remember why you wanted them. It will jog your memory when you're sorting through them later.
- If there's a printer-friendly option, use it. It will give you a print-out without unnecessary graphics or adverts.
- Check the bottom line of your print-outs. It should show the URL for that page of the website, and the date. You need those if you have to list your sources or if you want to quote from the page.

Researching by asking other people

You're likely to do this for two reasons:

- you need help from someone who knows a lot about a topic
- you need to find out several people's opinions on something.

TRY THIS

Go to page 98 to find out how to see how directory sites work.

TOP TIP

Bookmark sites you use regularly by adding the URL to your browser. How to do this will depend on which browser you use, eg Internet Explorer, Firefox.

Information from an expert

Explain politely why you are carrying out the investigation. Ask questions slowly and clearly about what they do and how they do it. If they don't mind, you could take written notes so you remember what they tell you. Put the name and title of the person, and the date, at the top. This is especially important if you might be seeing more than one person, to avoid getting your notes muddled up.

Ask whether you may contact them again, in case there's anything you need to check. Write down their phone number or email address. Above all, remember to say 'thank you'!

Case study: Asking for help

Linda is a Year 10 learner on the optional joinery unit of the BTEC First in Construction. She is struggling to draw a basic mortice and tenon joint in a theory lesson before constructing it for real in a practical lesson. Linda doesn't like to ask for help as she is fiercely independent and wants to get everything right first time.

However, she swallows her pride and asks her tutor, who is an experienced bench joiner, for some help with the joint. The tutor asks the whole group to come together and have a 'tool-box talk' about the correct construction of this joint. Having a class discussion means that Linda is not put on the spot or embarrassed in front of her peers. The talk goes well and it turns out Linda wasn't the only one who was not sure what to do!

Linda uses the knowledge she has gained in the next practical session, successfully marking out the mortice and tenon joint and asking her tutor when she needs help as she proceeds through the task. The tutor is delighted with her progress. Linda now uses this method of clarifying instructions and checking back during a task in other subjects, leading to a noticeable improvement in her academic results.

Often, you can find things out by asking someone who has more experience, qualifications and knowledge than you. Sometimes this is the best way of obtaining information quickly, easily and efficiently. The construction industry uses lots of technical words that you will need to learn and understand. Ask the meaning of anything you don't understand, or look up the words in a reference book.

The opinions of several people

The easiest way to do this is with a questionnaire. You can either give people the questionnaire to complete themselves or interview them and complete it yourself. Professional interviewers often telephone people to ask questions, but at this stage it's not a good idea unless you know the people you're phoning and they're happy for you to do this.

Devising a questionnaire

1   Make sure it has a title and clear instructions.

2   Rather than ask for opinions, give people options, eg yes/no, maybe/always, never/sometimes. This will make it easier to analyse the results.

3   Or you can ask interviewees to give a score, say out of 5, making it clear what each number represents, eg 5 = excellent, 4 = very good.

4   Keep your questionnaire short so that your interviewees don't lose interest. Between 10 and 15 questions is probably about right, as long as that's enough to find out all you need.

5   Remember to add 'thank you' at the end.

6   Decide upon the representative sample of people you will approach. These are the people whose views are the most relevant to the topic you're investigating.

7   Decide how many responses you need to get a valid answer. This means that the answer is representative of the wider population. For example, if you want views on food in your canteen, it's pointless only asking five people. You might pick the only five people who detest (or love) the food it serves.

TOP TIP

Design your questionnaire so that you get quantifiable answers. This means you can easily add them up to get your final result.

TRY THIS

Always test your draft questionnaire on several people, to highlight any confusing questions or instructions.

File management and keeping a logbook

To organise your work, you will need:

- a lever arch file
- file dividers for each unit
- a section for assignments
- an admin section for course-related material
- a section for your time table and assessment schedule.

Being organised will save you time and energy, allowing you to access the information you require for each lesson quickly and easily.

Personal Protective Equipment

You will need some **PPE** (Personal Protective Equipment) for the practical units of the BTEC First in Construction. For craft-related practical activities, you must wear safety footwear with steel toe caps to prevent injury to your toes and you will need to acquire a pair of overalls to keep your day clothes clean. You may also need safety spectacles for certain operations.

You should keep your PPE:

- clean
- washed
- in good working order.
- You should replace any item that is defective.

Observation records in a logbook

You will produce detailed records of your progress during practical workshops and the production of assessed pieces of work. The best way of doing this is to ask a colleague to photograph your work through its production. Remember to:

- save the digital photographs onto a disc or USB stick
- print a copy of the record
- get it signed and dated by a tutor
- file it within your folder of evidence or logbook
- ensure that the correct evidence is collected.

Activity: Researching brick bonds

Your tutor has asked you to produce some research on brick bonds for the brickwork unit.

For each type of bond shown in the table below, find a diagram. Complete the table by entering a drawing of the bond, and noting the source.

Bond	Diagram	Source
stretcher bond		
Flemish bond		
old English bond		

Managing your information

Whether you've found lots of information or only a little, assessing what you have and using it wisely is very important. This section will help you avoid the main pitfalls.

Organising and selecting your information

Organising your information

The first step is to organise your information so that it's easy to use.

- Make sure your written notes are neat and have a clear heading – it's often useful to date them, too.
- Note useful pages in any books or magazines you have borrowed.
- Highlight relevant parts of any handouts or leaflets.
- Work out the results of any questionnaires you've used.

Selecting your information

Re-read the **assignment brief** or instructions you were given to remind yourself of the exact wording of the question(s) and divide your information into three groups:

1 Information that is totally relevant.

2 Information that is not as good, but could come in useful.

3 Information that doesn't match the questions or assignment brief very much but that you kept because you couldn't find anything better!

Check there are no obvious gaps in your information against the questions or assignment brief. If there are, make a note of them so that you know exactly what you still have to find. Although it's ideal to have everything you need before you start work, don't delay if you're short of time.

Putting your information in order

Putting your information in a logical order means you can find what you want easily. It will save you time in the long run. This is doubly important if you have lots of information and will be doing the work over several sessions.

Good organisational skills are essential. A clean, tidy work area and a sensible filing system:

- allow quick access to resources
- save time and effort
- tell you what work you have to complete
- help you get good results!

Case study: Organising yourself

Sam is not very organised and his file is a complete mess. It has not been divided into units; he has just hole-punched notes as he has made them and placed them in the file in no particular order.

Sam suddenly realises that he is not doing well on his GCSE courses and that his BTEC First is equivalent to between two and four GCSEs. If he works hard to get merit and distinction grades, it will lift his overall academic performance allowing him to progress onto a Level 3 course at the local college.

Sam opens up his file to be met with a pile of paper that makes no sense. His notes are poorly written and are not marked with a unit or date to help him put them in order.

He realises that he will have to spend a considerable amount of time putting things into the right order, so he can find the information he needs to complete his assignments to a good standard.

Sam visits a local construction project. Here he is shown how the on-site filing system helps to control the flow of information, enabling the operatives to construct the project efficiently. It was explained that good filing is essential in order to avoid complicated and costly mistakes being made.

After Sam sees a real filing system in use, Sam decides to sort out his own filing by using file dividers to separate each construction unit.

Activity: Setting up a filing system

Set up your own filing system using an A4 lever arch file and dividers. Include the following:

- a course title page like the one shown on opposite
- a note of who the file belongs to, so if you lose it you can get it back
- a page outlining the structure of the units you are taking
- file dividers labelled with the title of each unit
- an assignments section
- a useful information section.

Activity: Making a contents page for your file

Photocopy this page, complete the details and put it in the front of your file.

This file belongs to me!

Put your school or college logo here.

Put your photo here.

Name ....

Course ....

Year ....

Year 1 Units ....

....

....

Year 2 Units ....

....

....

Course Tutor ....

Interpreting and presenting your information

The next stage is to use your information to prepare the document and/or oral presentation you have to give. There are four steps:

1 Understand what you're reading.

2 Interpret what you're reading.

3 Know the best form in which to produce the information, bearing in mind the purpose for which it is required.

4 Create the required document so that it's in a suitable layout with correct spelling and punctuation.

Understanding what you read

As a general rule, never use information that you don't understand. However, nobody understands complex or unfamiliar material the first time they read it, especially if they just scan through it quickly. Before you reject it, try this:

Read it once to get the main idea.	Read it again, slowly, to try to take in more detail.	Look up any words you don't know in a dictionary to find out what they mean.
Write your own version.	Summarise the main points in your own words.	Read it a third time and underline or highlight the main points. (If this is a book or magazine that you shouldn't write in, take a photocopy first and write on that.)

Special note: Show both the article and your own version to your tutor to check your understanding. This will help you identify any points you missed out and help you improve your skills of interpreting and summarising.

Understanding unfamiliar information

Interpreting what you read

Interpreting what you read is different from understanding it. This is because you can't always take it for granted that something you read means what it says. The writer may have had a very strong or biased opinion, or may have exaggerated for effect. This doesn't mean that you can't use the information, but that you will need to add an explanation.

Strong opinions and bias

People often have strong points of view about certain topics. This may be based on reliable facts, but not always! We can all jump to conclusions that may not be very logical, especially if we feel strongly about something.

Things aren't always what they seem to be. Are these boys fighting or are they having a good time?

Exaggeration

Many newspapers exaggerate facts to startle and attract their readers.

LOCAL FIRM DOUBLES STAFF IN TWO WEEKS!

This newspaper headline sounds very positive. You could easily think it means employment is growing and there are more jobs in your area. Then you read on, and find the firm had only four staff and now has eight!

Tables and graphs

You need to be able to interpret what the figures mean, especially when you look at differences between columns or rows. For example, your friend might have an impressive spreadsheet that lists his income and expenditure. In reality, it doesn't tell you much until you add the figures up and subtract one from the other. Only then can you say whether he is getting into debt. And even if he is, you need to see his budget over a few months, rather than just one which may be exceptional.

Choosing a format

You may have been given specific instructions about the format and layout of a document you have to produce, in which case life is easy as long as you follow them! If not, think carefully about the best way to set out your information so that it is clear.

TRY THIS

There are many scare stories in the media about issues such as immigration, children's reading ability or obesity. Next time you're watching television and these are discussed, see if you can spot biased views, exaggeration and claims without any supporting evidence.

TOP TIP

Never make assumptions or jump to conclusions. Make sure you have all the evidence to support your views.

Different formats	Example
text	when you write in paragraphs or prepare a report or summary
graphical	a diagram, graph or chart
pictorial	a drawing, photograph, cartoon or pictogram
tabular	numerical information in a table

The best method(s) will depend on the information you have, the source(s) of your material and the purpose of the document – a leaflet for schoolchildren needs graphics and pictures to make it lively, whereas a report to company shareholders would be mainly in text form with just one or two graphs.

Stating your sources

Whatever format you use, if you are including other people's views, comments or opinions, or copying a table or diagram from another publication, you must state the source by including the name of the author, publication or the web address. This can be in the text or as part of a list at the end. Failure to do this (so you are really pretending other people's work is your own) is known as **plagiarism**. Plagiarism is a serious offence with penalties to match.

Text format

Creating written documents gets easier with practice. These points should help.

TOP TIP

Don't just rely on your spellchecker. It won't find a word that is spelled wrongly but makes another valid word (eg from/form), so you must proofread everything. Remember to check whether it is set to check American English or British English. There are some spelling differences.

Golden rules for written documents

1. Think about who will be reading it, then write in an appropriate language and style.

2. Ensure it is technically correct, ie no wrong spellings or bad punctuation.

3. Take time to make it look good, with clear headings, consistent spacing and plenty of white space.

4. Write in paragraphs, each with a different theme. Leave a line space between each one.

5. If you have a lot of separate points to mention, use bullets or numbered points. Numbered points show a certain order or quantity (step 1, step 2, etc). Use bullet points when there is no suggested order.

6. Only use words that you understand the meaning of, or it might look as if you don't know what you mean.

7. Structure your document so that it has a beginning, middle and end.

8. Prepare a draft and ask your tutor to confirm you are on the right track and are using your information in the best way.

Activity: Structure a document

This activity is designed to show you how to structure a report; with an introduction, middle and summary. Write a short piece about how you coped with your first assignment using the table headings and questions for guidance.

Introduction How did you feel when you started the assignment? What were your expectations of the task?	
Middle What progress did you make on the task? How did your approach develop during the course of the assignment? How hard was it?	
Summary How much did you achieve? What grades did you get? What would you do differently to improve your performance in future assignments?	

Try this activity again after you have completed several more assignments.
Are you making progress in your approach to assignments?

Graphical format

Most people find graphics better than a long description for creating a quick picture in the viewer's mind. There are several types of graphical format, and you can easily produce any of these if you have good ICT skills.

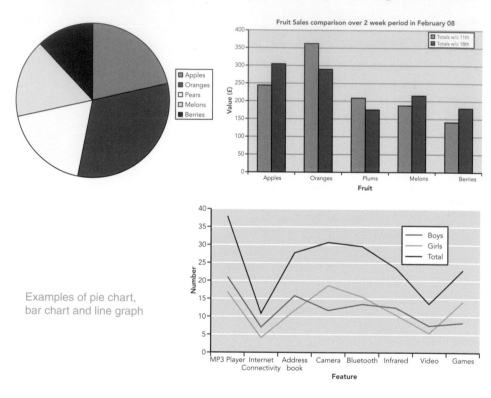

Examples of pie chart, bar chart and line graph

Pictorial format

Newspapers and magazines use pictures to illustrate situations and reduce the amount of words needed. It doesn't always have to be photographs though. For example, a new building may be sketched to show what it will look like.

A pictogram or pictograph is another type of pictorial format, such as charts which use the image of an object (fruit, coins, even pizzas) to represent data, such as the number eaten or amount spent.

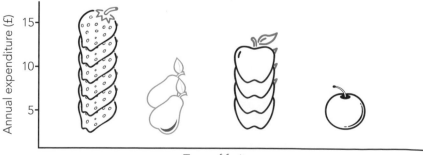

Tabular format

A table can be an easy way to communicate information. Imagine a retailer preparing information about the items in stock. Text would be difficult to understand and comparisons between stock levels and sales would be almost impossible to make. A table, however, would easily show the fastest-selling items.

Tables are also ideal if you are showing rankings – such as best-selling music or books.

Bestsellers list – September 2009

Position	Title	Author	Imprint	Publication
1 (New)	Lost Symbol,The	Brown, Dan	Bantam Press	15-Sep-2009
2 (1)	Complaints, The	Rankin, Ian	Orion	03-Sep-2009
3 (New)	Return Journey, The	Binchy, Maeve	Orion	17-Sep-2009
4 (7)	Sapphire	Price, Katie	Century	30-Jul-2009
5 (9)	Wolf Hall	Mantel, Hilary	Fourth Estate	30-Apr-2009
6 (3)	Week in December, A	Faulks, Sebastian	Hutchinson	03-Sep-2009
7 (2)	Alex Cross's Trial	Patterson, James	Century	10-Sep-2009
8 (4)	White Queen, The	Gregory, Philippa	Simon & Schuster Ltd	18-Aug-2009
9 (5)	Even Money	Francis, Dick & Francis, Felix	Michael Joseph	03-Sep-2009
10 (8)	206 Bones	Reichs, Kathy	William Heinemann	27-Aug-2009

National newspaper circulation – September 2009

	August 2009	August 2008	% change on last year	August 09 (without bulks)	March 2009 – August 2009	% change on last year
Sun	3,128,501	3,148,792	-0.64	3,128,501	3,052,480	-2.25
Daily Mail	2,171,686	2,258,843	-3.86	2,044,079	2,178,462	-4.45
Daily Mirror	1,324,883	1,455,270	-8.96	1,324,883	1,331,108	9.44
Daily Star	886,814	751,494	18.01	886,814	855,511	16.65
The Daily Telegraph	814,087	860,298	-5.37	722,644	807,328	-6.73
Daily Express	730,234	748,664	-2.46	730,234	727,824	-1.32
Times	576,185	612,779	-5.97	529,746	588,471	-4.63
Financial Times	395,845	417,570	-5.2	365,269	411,098	-6.7
Daily Record	347,302	390,197	-10.99	345,277	350,306	-10.59
Guardian	311,387	332,587	-6.37	311,387	332,790	-4.11
Independent	187,837	230,033	-18.34	148,551	198,445	-16.76

Activity: Using images to represent information

1 Try to find appropriate images to represent the construction terms listed in this table. Carefully cut out and paste photographs or other images into the table so it is neat and presentable.

Term	Image
sustainability	
renewable energy	
construction professional	
RIBA	
civil engineering	

2 Represent the information on the left of the table with a diagram, graph or chart.

Information	Diagram, graph or chart
housing output was 10 in January, 15 in February and 27 in March	
out of 100m² of brickwork laid, gang one laid 25m², gang two laid 50m² and gangs three and four laid 12.5m² each	
a joiner worked 3 hours on job one, 2 hours on job two, 5 hours on job three and 16 hours on job four, and is paid £12 per hour	

Making presentations

Presentations help you to learn communication skills.

Some people hate the idea of standing up to speak in front of an audience. This is quite normal, and you can use the extra energy from nerves to improve your performance.

Presentations aren't some form of torture devised by your tutor! They are included in your course because they help you learn many skills, such as speaking in public and preparing visual aids. They also help you practise working as a team member and give you a practical reason for researching information. And it can be far more enjoyable to talk about what you've found out rather than write about it!

There's a knack to preparing and giving a presentation so that you use your energies well, don't waste time, don't fall out with everyone around you and keep your stress levels as low as possible. Think about the task in three stages: preparation, organisation and delivery.

Preparation

Start your initial preparations as soon as you can. Putting them off will only cause problems later. Discuss the task in your team so that everyone is clear about what has to be done and how long you have to do it in.

Divide any research fairly among the team, allowing for people's strengths and weaknesses. You'll also need to agree:
- which visual aids would be best
- which handouts you need and who should prepare them
- where and when the presentation will be held, and what you should wear
- what questions you might be asked, both individually and as a team, and how you should prepare for them.

Once you've decided all this, carry out the tasks you've been allocated to the best of your ability and by the deadline agreed.

Organisation

This is about the planning you need to do as a team so that everything will run smoothly on the day.

Delivery

This refers to your performance during the presentation. Being well prepared and well organised helps stop you panicking. If you're very nervous at the start, take a few deep breaths and concentrate on the task, not yourself. It's quite normal to be nervous at the start but this usually fades once you get under way. You might even enjoy it …

Case study: Presenting your results

Ajura is taking part in a team presentation to her class on an unfamiliar aspect of construction: the construction of concrete foundations and their function. Each team has been given a different type of foundation to discuss: strip, pad and mass trench fill.

The presentation has been playing on Ajura's mind for the last two weeks and she finds that her fellow team members also feel anxious about public speaking. They decide to talk to the student support adviser, who helps with pastoral support for students.

She advises the team that everyone listening to their presentation will be feeling nervous about their own performance. She suggests they introduce some humour at the beginning in the form of an ice breaker which will settle everyone down and make the delivery easier.

The group take this on board and prepare very well for the presentation by practising repeatedly in front of friends and family until each person gets their section right and the whole delivery runs smoothly. Although their parents do not know anything about foundations, they seem to understand the message the team is trying to get across, giving everyone a bit of confidence.

On the day of the presentation, Ajura's group starts off well with a good, clear, introduction followed by an interactive middle section involving the audience, and concluding with a final summary. They present some photographs of foundations and this goes down well with the audience.

When asked how they felt about the experience, the general feeling was that all the practice really paid off, making them more comfortable and allowing them to enjoy the experience.

TOP TIP

Never read from prepared prompt cards! Look at the audience when you're talking and smile occasionally. If you need to use prompt cards as a reminder, make sure they are clear so that you need only glance at them.

TOP TIP

Remember, the audience always makes allowances for some nerves!

TOP TIP

When making a PowerPoint presentation, don't just read out what it says on the slides. The audience can read! Use the slides as prompt cards.

Activity: Getting organised for your presentation

A good presentation depends on one thing, and that is careful planning. Select a specification topic area and use the following form to identify the planning issues for delivering a presentation. After the presentation, complete the feedback box to help you pinpoint areas for improvement.

Part of presentation	Ask yourself...	Planning required
before the presentation	How will we divide the research?	
introduction – setting the scene for the topic	How long will the intro be? Will we use photographs? What form of presentation shall we use? Do we need IT? Who will deliver the intro?	
main delivery	How much material? What format? What IT equipment? How many photographs? Who will deliver what? Can we put the material into our own words? What level of language shall we use? Length of presentation?	
final summary	What are the main points to summarise? Who will deliver this section? Do we need handouts?	
		Review and feedback
after the presentation	What went well? What did not go so well? Was the presentation the right length? Did everyone understand the main message?	

Your assessments

The importance of assignments

All learners on BTEC First courses are assessed by means of **assignments**. Each one is designed to link to specific **learning outcomes** and **grading criteria**. At the end of the course, your assignment grades put together determine your overall grade.

To get the best grade you can, you need to know the golden rules that apply to all assignments, then how to interpret the specific instructions.

10 golden rules for assignments

1. Check that you understand the instructions.

2. Check whether you have to do all the work on your own, or if you will do some as a member of a group. If you work as a team, you need to identify which parts are your own contributions.

3. Always write down any verbal instructions you are given.

4. Check the final deadline and any penalties for not meeting it.

5. Make sure you know what to do if you have a serious personal problem, eg illness, and need an official extension.

6. Copying someone else's work (**plagiarism**) is a serious offence and is easy for experienced tutors to spot. It's never worth the risk.

7. Schedule enough time for finding out the information and doing initial planning.

8. Allow plenty of time between talking to your tutor about your plans, preparations and drafts and the final deadline.

9. Don't panic if the assignment seems long or complicated. Break it down into small, manageable chunks.

10. If you suddenly get stuck, ask your tutor to talk things through with you.

Case study: Planning to get good results

Sied wants to do well on his BTEC First in Construction as he would like to go on to National Level before undertaking a university degree. He is planning ahead to ensure he achieves his eventual goal.

If he can get through the next four years of study, Sied will be the first in his family to attend university. He wants to go to Nottingham University which has a large faculty of construction and numerous construction degree courses. He is aware that the competition for places is fierce and he will need distinctions at National Level to progress to higher education. Starting as he means to go on, Said wants to see if he can obtain distinctions at Level 2.

Sied has been given his first assignment for the Construction Technology Methods unit. It contains two pass criteria, one merit and

one distinction. The tutor has explained that there will be two assignments per unit on the course and that, in order to receive an overall distinction award for the qualification, learners have to complete all the pass, merit and distinction criteria. Sied realises that it is going to be hard to obtain a distinction, but he has come up with a plan: he will complete the pass criteria for each assignment in the first week that it is issued, thus giving him more time to devote to the merit and distinction criteria.

Sied has also set aside some time at weekends in order to complete this task. He hands in the first assignment and three weeks later is delighted to obtain his first distinction. His planning and time spent understanding the assessment structure mean he has the tools he needs to achieve what he wants.

Activity: Understanding your course specification

Take a close look at your course specification and for each unit identify how many pass, merit and distinction criteria there are. For each unit, draw up a table like the one shown below.

Unit number and title	Pass	Date	Merit	Date	Distinction	Date

As you complete each criterion, enter the date into the table. You now have a planning document which will also allow you to track your progress.

Interpreting the instructions

Most assignments start with a **command word** – describe, explain, evaluate, etc. These words relate to how complex the answer should be.

Command words

Learners often don't do their best because they read the command words but don't understand exactly what they have to do. The tables on the following pages show you what is required for each grade when you see a particular command word.

Command words and obtaining a pass

Complete ...	Complete a form, diagram or drawing.
Demonstrate ...	Show that you can do a particular activity.
Describe ...	Give a clear, straightforward description that includes all the main points.
Identify ...	Give all the basic facts relating to a certain topic.
List ...	Write a list of the main items (not sentences).
Name ...	State the proper terms related to a drawing or diagram.
Outline ...	Give all the main points, but without going into too much detail.
State ...	Point out or list the main features.

Examples:

- **List** the main features on your mobile phone.
- **Describe** the best way to greet a customer.
- **Outline** the procedures you follow to keep your computer system secure.

Command words and obtaining a merit

Analyse ...	Identify the factors that apply, and state how these are linked and how each of them relates to the topic.
Comment on ...	Give your own opinions or views.
Compare ... Contrast ...	Identify the main factors relating to two or more items and point out the similarities and differences.
Competently use ...	Take full account of information and feedback you have obtained to review or improve an activity.
Demonstrate ...	Prove you can carry out a more complex activity.
Describe ...	Give a full description including details of all the relevant features.
Explain ...	Give logical reasons to support your views.
Justify ...	Give reasons for the points you are making so that the reader knows what you're thinking.
Suggest ...	Give your own ideas or thoughts.

Examples:

- **Explain** why mobile phones are so popular.
- **Describe** the needs of four different types of customers.
- **Suggest** the type of procedures your employer would need to introduce to keep the IT system secure.

TRY THIS

Check the command word you are likely to see for each of your units in the **grading grid** in advance. This tells you the **grading criteria** for the unit so that you know the evidence you will have to present.

Command words and obtaining a distinction

Analyse ...	Identify several relevant factors, show how they are linked, and explain the importance of each.
Compare ... **Contrast ...**	Identify the main factors in two or more situations, then explain the similarities and differences, and in some cases say which is best and why.
Demonstrate ...	Prove that you can carry out a complex activity taking into account information you have obtained or received to adapt your original idea.
Describe ...	Give a comprehensive description which tells a story to the reader and shows that you can apply your knowledge and information correctly.
Evaluate ...	Bring together all your information and make a judgement on the importance or success of something.
Explain ...	Provide full details and reasons to support the arguments you are making.
Justify ...	Give full reasons or evidence to support your opinion.
Recommend ...	Weigh up all the evidence to come to a conclusion, with reasons, about what would be best.

Examples:

● **Evaluate** the features and performance of your mobile phone.

● **Analyse** the role of customer service in contributing to an organisation's success.

● **Justify** the main features on the website of a large, successful organisation of your choice.

TOP TIP

Think of assignments as an opportunity to demonstrate what you've learned and to get useful feedback about your work.

Activity: Practice questions

1 Try this practice question at merit level.

'The Ministry of Defence and an independent company both issue work to the construction industry in the UK. Compare and contrast the needs of these two construction clients.'

Client 1

Client 2

2 To achieve a distinction criterion requires demonstration of higher level skills.

'Justification' is often the key requirement of this level of grading. 'To justify' means to give a full reason in support of the opinion presented. Try the exercises below to see how well you get on.

a) Justify membership of a professional association in construction.

_____

_____

_____

_____

_____

b) Justify your reasons for wanting to get high grades.

_____

_____

_____

_____

_____

c) Justify the training and qualifications that may be required to undertake a craft role in construction.

_____

_____

_____

_____

_____

TOP TIP

When presenting evidence for assessment, think about the person who will be looking through it. Make sure that your 'pitch' is well planned and that it is easy for the assessor to match your evidence against the grading criteria.

Sample assignment

Front sheet

Make sure that all the boxes on the front sheet are completed, including your name.

Ensure you hand in your work on time. Make sure you know your centre's rules on this.

Ask your tutor to feedback on any draft work before the submission to ensure that you have answered the tasks correctly and in the format required to meet the assessment criteria.

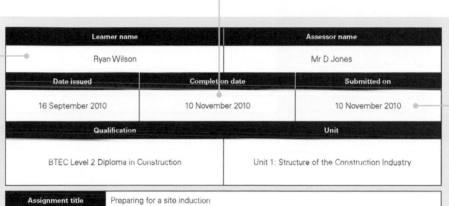

Learner name	Assessor name
Ryan Wilson	Mr D Jones

Date issued	Completion date	Submitted on
16 September 2010	10 November 2010	10 November 2010

Qualification	Unit
BTEC Level 2 Diploma in Construction	Unit 1: Structure of the Construction Industry

Assignment title	Preparing for a site induction

In this assessment you will have opportunities to provide evidence against the following criteria.
Indicate the page numbers where the evidence can be found.

Criteria reference	To achieve the criteria the evidence must show that the student is able to:	Task no.	Page numbers
P4	identify the personnel working in the construction industry	1	1
P5	describe the roles and responsibilities of the personnel working in the construction industry	2	2–5
P6	identify the qualifications, training and development needed to support careers in the construction industry	3	6
M3	explain how operatives and crafts persons can develop their careers and progress to a technical or professional role in a given area of activity	4	7–8
D2	evaluate two different organisational frameworks in terms of how they affect the interactions between members of the construction team	5	9–11

Learner declaration

I certify that the work submitted for this assignment is my own and research sources are fully acknowledged.

Learner signature: *Ryan Wilson*   Date: *10 November 2010*

Sign the declaration to show the work is yours.

The work you present must be in your own words. Anything that you have copied and used must be acknowledged with its source.

Ensure that you meet the evidence requirements for each assessed criteria. Ask your tutor if you are unsure whether your evidence meets the criteria as there may be different forms of evidence that are acceptable.

This table informs you of the criteria that are being assessed and allows you to enter the page numbers where you have provided evidence for each criterion.

Assignment brief

The scenario is essential. It sets the assignment in a real, vocational context.

The title is important. Always structure your work so it fits under this assessment title. Don't stray into other topic areas.

Unit title	Unit 1: Structure of the Construction Industry
Qualification	BTEC Level 2 Diploma in Construction
Start date	16 September 2010
Deadline date	10 November 2010
Assessor	Mr D Jones

Assignment title	Preparing for a site induction

The purpose of this assignment is to:
Allow you to demonstrate your knowledge and understanding of the human resources in the construction industry and of careers in the construction industry.

Scenario
You are working as a trainee site manager for a medium-size construction company. The Site Manager has asked for you to support her in inducting ten new apprentices who have recently been employed by the company. First of all she wants you to prepare a report using text, tables, charts, images and diagrams where appropriate, and provide information which will help new apprentices starting with the company. Your report will be included in the company's new induction handbook.

Task 1
Your company employs a representative cross-section of personnel working in the construction industry, including operative, craftsperson, technical, supervisory, managerial, and professional personnel.

Identify two personnel working in the construction industry from the following classifications:

- operative
- craft
- technical
- supervisory
- managerial
- professional

This provides evidence for P4

Task 2
Using the personnel that you have identified in Task 1, describe their roles and responsibilities whilst working in the construction industry.

This provides evidence for P5

Task 3
Identify the

- qualifications
- training
- and development

needed to support three careers in the construction industry for three of the categories of personnel that you identified in Task 1.

This provides evidence for P6

The command word here is 'identify'. This means to list, not to describe, so you could produce a bullet point list.

The command word here is 'describe'. This needs than just listing. You need to provide a more detailed description.

The command word here is 'explain'. This involves discussing the issue or problem in detailed language that can be clearly understood.

The command word here is 'evaluate'. This involves weighing up the advantages and disadvantages.

Task 4

Several construction site personnel have approached you as the site manager on the current construction project and have asked for information on how they can become a qualified site manager.

Explain how

- *operatives* and
- *craftspersons*

can develop their careers and progress to a technical or professional role in a given area of activity.

This provides evidence for M3

Task 5

Evaluate the organisational frameworks of two rival construction companies, one large and one medium-sized. If possible these should be locally based. You should identify the lines of communication and line management responsibility (direct and lateral) within these companies and describe how each system affects the interactions between members of the construction team.

This provides evidence for D2

Sources of information

See Appendixes 1 and 2 for construction company profiles that could be used for Task 5, should you be unable to gain access to local construction companies.

Books

Chudley R and Greeno R — *Advanced Construction Technology, 4th Edition* (Pearson, 2006) ISBN 9780132019859

Chudley R and Greeno R — *Building Construction Handbook, 7th Edition* (Butterworth-Heinemann, 2008) ISBN 9780750686228

Langston C A Y, Craig A and Ding G K C — *Sustainable Practices in the Built Environment, 2nd Edition* (Butterworth-Heinemann, 2001) ISBN 0750651539

Manley S, Charters M, Francis C, Topliss S, Doyle M — *Construction and the Built Environment* (Pearson, 2008) ISBN 9780435499914

Osbourn D and Greeno R — *Introduction to Building, 3rd Edition* (Pearson, 2002) ISBN 0582473039

Journals

Construction News (see www.cnplus.co.uk)
Building magazine (see www.building.co.uk)

Websites

www.architecture.com RIBA Royal Institute of British Architects
www.ciob.org.uk CIOB Chartered Institute of Building
www.communities.gov.uk
www.rics.org RICS Royal Institute of Chartered Surveyors

This brief has been verified as being fit for purpose			
Assessor	Mr D Jones		
Signature	D Jones	Date	25 September 2010
Internal verifier	Mr Michael Smith		
Signature	M Smith	Date	25 September 2010

Supplementary material

APPENDIX 1

Complex Construction Ltd – Company Profile

Complex Construction Ltd is the award-winning leader in the delivery of community regeneration and complex housing projects, delivering thousands of new and improved homes across northern England.

Overseen by our Chairman Sir Gary Hoggrite, we employ approximately 60 employees. Below is a list of the staff we currently employ. These are supported by various self-employed crafts and trades people.

- Managing Director
- Quality Consultant
- Health and Safety Advisor
- Contracts Director
- Estimating Director
- Business Development Manager
- Estimator/Surveyor
- Management Accountant (Wages Clerk and Accountant)
- Office Manager (office assistants)
- Company Secretary
- Contracts Manager (overseeing various construction trades, Operatives and a Contracts Administrator)

Working in partnership with a wide range of governmental agencies and private businesses, Complex Construction Ltd provides new and improved homes as part of a comprehensive and flexible package of housing support services to help build strong, dynamic and sustainable communities.

We are also playing a major role in delivering sustainable communities by helping to bring all social housing up to the Government's Decent Homes Standard by 2010, delivering well-designed, eco-friendly and competitively priced homes, and bring new life to previously run-down local communities.

Overall, the most important challenge for us is to adapt continually as a business in response to the requirements of the market, and to help create a range of innovative solutions to support our partners in regenerating communities and delivering a positive and lasting legacy for the future. Our partnership approach is one of the hallmarks of the way we do business.

Complex Construction Ltd has an excellent regional reputation for successfully delivering challenging schemes and complex projects. Whether we are involved in new build or renovations to listed buildings, work in town centres or conservation areas, Complex Construction Ltd has a 'can do' attitude, enabling delivery of projects on time and on budget.

At Complex Construction Ltd, we recognise that the performance of our employees is central to the success of our business. We are committed to creating a working environment in which each employee is able to make their full contribution to our success and encouraged to reach their full potential.

Complex Construction Ltd is an equal opportunity employer. We recruit, train, develop and promote staff solely on the basis of merit, consistent with our business goals. We especially value the contribution that individuals of different backgrounds, cultures and abilities can bring to their work with us. We are continually striving to build a workforce which is truly representative of the increasingly diverse communities in which we serve and work. We do not tolerate discrimination in the workplace. In recruitment and promotion no one is disadvantaged by considerations of age, gender, sexual orientation, marital status, colour, race, nationality, ethnic or national origins, religion or disability, which cannot be justified. We conduct systematic reviews to ensure that we meet these goals and the legal obligations that support them.

Representatives of Complex Construction Ltd's senior management meet regularly with colleagues from other companies as part of a regional Equal Opportunities and Diversity Group to consider best practice in all areas of business and to strive for continuous improvement.

APPENDIX 2

International Homes Ltd – Company Profile

International Homes Ltd was established in 1902 and has an unparalleled record in the construction industry both nationally and internationally Today the company has an annual turnover of in excess of £150 million. The company draws on over an hundred years of quality homebuilding experience to consistently meet the expectations of the modern market. We aim to be at the forefront of setting industry standards in customer care.

International Homes Ltd is led by Managing Director Alison Mayfield, who heads up a well-organised management team responsible for a workforce of approximately 180 employees. The management team head up departments in the following areas:

- Quality control and assurance
- Health and safety
- Contracts management (overseeing Site Managers, Engineers, Technicians, various Craft/Trade Operatives and General Operatives)
- Commercial
- Surveying
- Finance and administration

This organisational infrastructure equips and enables us to respond to contractual challenges of regional, national and international scale.

International Homes Ltd's portfolio demonstrates remarkable diversity in its homebuilding record. Developments across Europe, from Scotland to Italy, show a wide range of new homes, from one bedroom apartments and starter homes to large, detached family homes for every taste and budget.

In respect of International Homes' environmental record, the company follows the following straightforward guidelines:

- *We design developments in harmony with their immediate natural environment.* To protect the natural environment that surrounds a new site, we survey each area intensively. We can then layout the development around its natural features.
- *We re-use previously built-on land wherever we can.* To keep the acquisition and development of greenfield sites to a minimum, we aim to renovate old buildings and renew previous developments wherever we can, re-using as much brownfield land for our new developments as possible.
- *We build energy-efficient homes.* It is always our aim and approach to use the latest techniques in building energy efficient new homes.
- *We use low-waste, sustainable, eco-friendly materials whenever we can.* For example, we try to use timber from sustainable and carefully managed plantations. We favour non-toxic water-based paints. We try to use aggregate from the nearest pits to keep the cost of supply, environmentally as well as economically, to a minimum.
- *We recycle our waste efficiently.* In our on-site waste processing, we strive to be effective recyclers; where we have to resort to off-site waste management, we return pallets and containers to carefully sourced suppliers of efficient skip management.

Equality of opportunity is also important to us. International Homes Ltd is committed to being an equal opportunities employer and to ensuring that all employees, job applicants, contractors and customers are treated fairly and are not subject to discrimination. We therefore promote equality of opportunity in the recruitment, appraisal, training, development and promotion of our staff, all of whom are engaged with on the basis of their relative merits and abilities.

We aim to ensure that current and potential employees are offered the same opportunities regardless of their race, religion, nationality, ethnic origin, age, sex, sexual orientation, marital status, disability, or any other characteristic unrelated to the performance of their jobs.

Sample learner work

The standard of evidence here could be improved by giving more detailed description in this table of what the roles include.

Specific job roles could have been given in these cases to improve the evidence further.

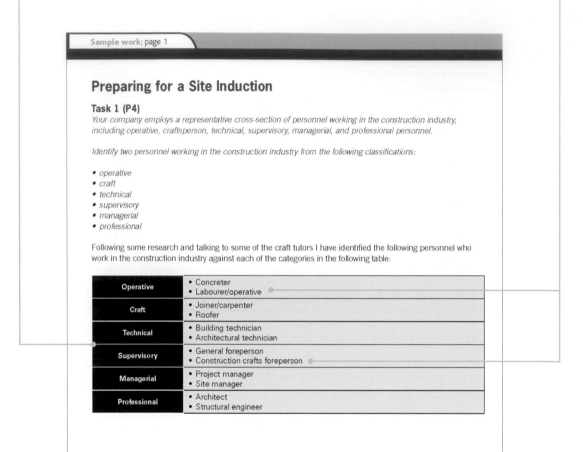

Sample work: page 1

Preparing for a Site Induction

Task 1 (P4)

Your company employs a representative cross-section of personnel working in the construction industry, including operative, craftsperson, technical, supervisory, managerial, and professional personnel.

Identify two personnel working in the construction industry from the following classifications:

- *operative*
- *craft*
- *technical*
- *supervisory*
- *managerial*
- *professional*

Following some research and talking to some of the craft tutors I have identified the following personnel who work in the construction industry against each of the categories in the following table:

Operative	• Concreter • Labourer/operative
Craft	• Joiner/carpenter • Roofer
Technical	• Building technician • Architectural technician
Supervisory	• General foreperson • Construction crafts foreperson
Managerial	• Project manager • Site manager
Professional	• Architect • Structural engineer

Make sure you get your technical terms correct. Cement is not prepared: it is mixed with sand and aggregate to make mortar, or concrete.

Sample work: page 2

Task 2 (P5)

*Using the job titles and roles identified in Task 1, select **two different** examples of company personnel from each of the categories below and describe their roles and responsibilities.*
- *operative*
- *craftsperson*
- *technical*
- *supervisory*
- *managerial*
- *professional*

Operative

Labourer/Operative: Construction labourers usually work 39 hours a week, Monday to Friday. Overtime is common due to the nature of the work they will carry out; for example a labourer working with a bricklayer would be expected to have mortar and bricks ready for the bricklayer to use so may have to start work early. Construction operatives mainly work outside, the work is very physical, and involves loading, unloading and storing materials. Their tasks include:
- preparing the ground for construction work;
- helping to set out areas to be dug for foundations and drains;
- preparing materials such as cement and plaster;
- digging shallow trenches;
- erecting and dismantling timbering used to support trenches;
- putting up hoardings, safety signs, barriers and site huts;
- road and pavement construction.

Concreter: Concreters use traditional hand tools such as picks and shovels, trowels and straight edges and machinery such as drills, cement mixers, vibrators and rollers. Working hours depend upon the job and vary considerably. Concreters usually work about 37 hours a week. This can include some early starts and late finishes. Their tasks include:
- preparing the appropriate areas for concreting by leveling and compacting the ground;
- taking delivery of the concrete;
- laying the concrete;
- compacting the concrete so that it is strong and durable;
- curing the concrete by wrapping or covering it in polythene sheeting.

Craftsperson

Carpenter/Joiner: The usual working week is 39 hours, Monday to Friday. Many jobs involve travelling to different sites, sometimes with time away from home. Carpenters spend a lot of time standing, bending, kneeling or crouching. Outdoors it can be cold and windy, and the work can involve climbing ladders and working on scaffolding. Bench joiners work in workshops and their work mainly consists of making items which a carpenter then fits on site. There are four different types of carpenter/joiner:
1. Bench joiners, who are mostly based in workshops, using woodworking tools and machinery to make parts such as doors, roof timbers and skirting boards;
2. Site carpenters, who work on site, fitting the prefabricated parts into buildings;
3. Shop-fitters, who specialise in producing and fitting shop fronts and interiors;
4. Formwork carpenters, who make moulds (formwork) for concrete structures, such as pillars for motorways and multi-storey car parks, bridges, suspended floors and staircases.

Roofer: Roofers build, maintain and repair roofs on houses, factories, offices, public buildings, shopping malls, and stadiums. They work with many different roofing materials, including concrete tiles, grey slate, sheeting and even thatch (thatching is a specialised craft). The working week is normally 37.5 hours, but it may be necessary to work overtime in the evenings and weekends. Self-employed roofers often work additional hours. Roofers work outdoors and at heights, and use ladders and scaffolding. The work is physically demanding, and roofers may have to work in cold and dirty conditions.

Be specific. A carpenter works with timber and a joiner joins timber together. They are two separate roles.

Keep your descriptions simple and easy to understand. This one could be clearer.

There are two types of roof: flat and pitched (sloped). Roofers can work on both types, or specialise. For example:

- Roof slaters and tilers lay new roofs and also replace broken slates and tiles on existing roofs.
- Built-up bituminous roofing involves putting layers of felt on top of each other, and using a blowlamp to melt bitumen on the back of the felt as it is laid.
- Single-ply roofing is where PVC sheeting (or a similar type) is used to cover the roof.
- Lead sheet is used as a weatherproof shield for flashing weatherings. It can be used on houses, as well as for unusual shapes such as spires.

Technical

Building Technician: Building technicians are involved in the construction of buildings and building works. They may also attend meetings between contractors, building inspectors and clients, measure and prepare a site for construction, supervise craftworkers and operatives on site, and be responsible for the timing and progress of the work. The standard working week is 37 to 40 hours, but building technicians often have to work overtime in the evening and at weekends. They work in an office or on site, depending on their job. Construction sites can be dirty, dusty, and noisy. Technicians may have to climb ladders and scaffolding or go underground. They may be involved in:

- drawing up plans for use by senior construction and surveying staff;
- estimating (detailing all the thousands of items needed for a contract);
- purchasing (buying the materials needed at the best price and quality);
- checking materials and equipment when they are delivered on site.

Architectural Technician: Architectural technicians/technologists work closely with architects and other building professionals, providing architectural design services and solutions on construction projects. Architectural technicians and technologists usually work from 9 am to 5 pm from Monday to Friday, although overtime may be necessary to meet deadlines. There is a limited amount of part-time work. Most work is based in the office, with some time spent visiting clients and sites. Site work may involve working outdoors in all weather conditions.

- They negotiate projects, assessing the needs of clients and users, and agree the project brief.
- They may then design the project, preparing and presenting design proposals using computer-aided design (CAD) and traditional methods.
- They may manage projects, obtaining and evaluating tenders and contracts.
- Architectural technicians/technologists also evaluate and advise on refurbishment, repair, reuse, recycling, and deconstruction of buildings.
- An architectural technologist has a broader range of skills than a technician, and will contribute more to the design and construction process, including contract management, certification and post-construction work.

Supervisory

General Foreperson: The General Foreperson provides leadership and is responsible for:

- scheduling work
- workface planning
- coordinating and supervising staff
- assisting in cost control
- ensuring the safety
- consistent and fair application of all Labour Relations policies and procedures
- providing apprentice training
- ensuring productivity of crews at the workface who install/assemble components of industrial products and structures.

The General Foreperson plays a big part in the relationship with the contractor, sub-contractors, company and client, and will be involved in all site meetings.

The impact of the size of the contractor and the type of work on the foreperson's role could have been made clearer.

Construction Crafts Foreperson: The Construction Crafts Foreperson provides leadership and schedules, coordinates, supervises, and ensures the safety and productivity of construction crafts staff who install/ assemble components onsite. The Crafts Foreperson is a key link person between the contractor, company and client. The foreperson liaises with management and sometimes the client onsite.

Managerial

Project Manager: Many construction project managers work in private organisations, such as large construction and development companies or consultancies. Some are employed by Government departments and others are self-employed. A construction project manager may perform the following tasks:
- interpret plans and estimate costs and quantities of materials needed;
- plan construction methods and procedures;
- coordinate the supply of labour and materials;
- supervise construction sites and direct site managers and subcontractors to make sure standards of building performance, quality, cost, schedules and safety are maintained;
- study building contract documents and negotiate with building owners and subcontractors;
- control preparation of cost estimates and the documentation for contract bids;
- control payment to subcontractors by valuation of completed works;
- make sure that building regulations, standards and by-laws are enforced in building operations;
- consult with architects, engineers and other technical workers to make sure that design intentions are met.

Site Manager: Site managers supervise and direct operations on a construction project to ensure it is completed safely, on time and within budget. This may be the construction of a new building or buildings, or the maintenance and refurbishment of existing ones. On smaller sites, managers may carry sole responsibility for the whole project; on larger sites, they may be in charge of a particular section, reporting to the senior site manager. Senior construction managers may oversee several construction projects at the same time. Their duties include:
- liaising with architects, planners, estimators and buyers prior to commencement of building work;
- planning a work schedule for the project using management software packages;
- preparing the construction site, including hire of labour, installation of temporary offices and overseeing delivery of materials;
- liaising with the site workforce;
- monitoring building progress, in particular, quality of work, compliance with regulations, costs and speed of completion of stages;
- reporting regularly to the client.

Professional

Architect: Architects work in the construction industry designing new buildings, restoring and conserving old buildings and developing new ways of using existing buildings. They are involved in construction projects from the earliest stages right through to completion. Architects usually work 9 am to 5 pm, from Monday to Friday. Most architects' work is office-based, although some time is spent visiting clients and sites. Their work includes:
- preparing and presenting design proposals to clients;
- advising clients;
- producing detailed drawings;
- negotiating with contractors and other professionals;
- attending regular meetings with clients, contractors and other specialists;
- coordinating the work of contractors;
- making site visits to check on progress;
- dealing with problems that might come up during building.

Structural Engineer: Structural engineers are involved in the design and construction of a range of structures, including large buildings, bridges and tunnels. They often work alongside architects, and are responsible for working out how buildings will be made to stand up to the stresses and strains placed upon them. A full-time structural engineer normally works 40 hours a week, Monday to Friday. Weekend work may occasionally be

Sample work: page 5

required. The work is office-based, but site visits can take place outside in all weather conditions. Travelling from site to site is common, and a driving licence is useful. Tasks and duties may include:

- preparing drawings and building specifications;
- investigating ground conditions and analysing results of site tests;
- calculating the loads and stresses placed upon structures;
- testing models on the computer to ensure that the structure can withstand forces such as wind, gravity and earth tremors;
- visiting sites to check that the construction is in accordance with the design.

The table format is clear and easy to understand, but more detail could be given on the development of the roles chosen.

Sample work: page 6

Task 3 (P6)

Identify the
- *qualifications*
- *training*
- *and development*

needed to support three careers in the construction industry for three of the categories of personnel that you identified in Task 1.

I have identified the following careers in the construction industry and explained for each what qualifications, training and development is required.

Career	Category	Qualifications	Training	Development
Bricklayer	Craft	NVQ Level 1 to 3	Health and Safety CSCS Card – Craft Plant handling COSHH Manual Handling	Experience in supervisory roles Ganger General Foreperson Assistant Site Manager
CAD Technician	Technical	National Diploma National Certificate HNC HND	Experience CAD CIOB Site Management	Progression through to professional role Experience in the industry
Structural Engineer	Professional	Degree Post Graduate Qualification	Working Experience Auto Cad ITC Skills	Membership of a professional association

Giving an example of the actual professional association would strengthen the evidence even further (e.g. RIBA).

Watch out for technical titles if you want your work to look professional. 'Surveying Technician' should be 'Assistant Quantity Surveyor'.

Task 4 (M3)
Several construction site personnel have approached you as the site manager on the current construction project and have asked for information on how they can become a qualified site manager.

Explain how
- *operatives and*
- *craftspersons*

can develop their careers and progress to a technical or professional role in a given area of activity.

Labourer to Surveying Technician
To enable a labourer to progress to become a surveying technician, he or she must possess good maths, IT and science skills, or be prepared to improve them by possibly completing GCSEs or A-levels to ensure they meet the entry requirements for a Level 4 construction course. It is also possible for the labourer to achieve a craft trade qualification such as an NVQ Level 2 and 3, which would help with progression. When they have got the required entry requirements, the labourer can study a NVQ at Level 4 in Quantity Surveying Practice, Valuation, Spatial Data Management or Town Planning, usually while in employment, or by taking an HNC/HND or Foundation degree course (either full-time or part-time). It would also be important that his or her employer is able to provide work experience as a surveying technician to enable links between the on- and off-the-job training. The Chartered Surveyors Training Trust offers work-based routes. Having completed either a relevant HNC/HND course or Foundation degree, surveying technicians can qualify as Technical Members of the Royal Institution of Chartered Surveyors by taking two years of structured training at work. It is important that continuous professional development and updating is carried out. Surveying technicians may have some opportunities for promotion or to specialise. They may gain more qualifications and become chartered surveyors. There are good opportunities for working abroad and self-employment is also possible.

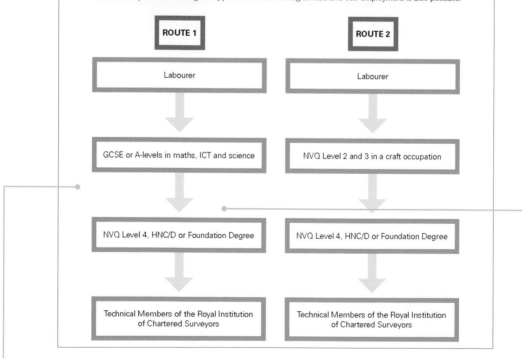

Don't be afraid to bring your own experience into your assignments. The BTEC First and National qualification routes might have been used here.

The Level 3 entrance qualifications required before starting the HNC/D should be mentioned here.

Sample work: page 8

Bricklayer to Architect

A fully qualified bricklayer will be qualified to NVQ Level 3 so the first step for the bricklayer would be to enroll onto the HNC/D in Construction. He or she would then need to complete a degree at a school of architecture, and gain experience in an architect's office. Mature applicants may be accepted for courses without the usual qualifications. The Royal Institute of British Architects (RIBA) offers an alternate training route for office-based candidates. To practice and use the title 'architect', individuals must register with the Architects Registration Board. This means spending at least seven years in training and higher education.

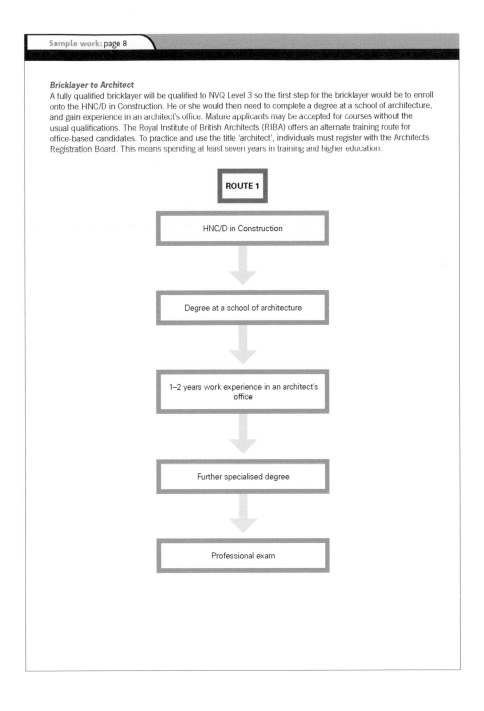

ROUTE 1

HNC/D in Construction

↓

Degree at a school of architecture

↓

1–2 years work experience in an architect's office

↓

Further specialised degree

↓

Professional exam

You should choose your companies carefully. Here you need to make sure they have enough differences to allow you to compare them effectively.

Sample work: page 9

Task 5 (D2)

Evaluate the organisational frameworks of two rival construction companies, one large and one medium-sized. If possible these should be locally based. You should identify the lines of communication and line management responsibility (direct and lateral) within these companies and describe how each system affects the interactions between members of the construction team.

As a medium-sized construction company, BuildRight International Ltd has two main local competitors within the industry: Complex Construction Ltd, which, as a medium-sized construction company with approximately 60 employees, has obvious similarities with BuildRight, and International Homes Ltd, a large construction company with approximately 180 employees. Because the great majority of construction companies (93 per cent) are classified as small businesses (between 1 and 13 employees) and these companies don't generally compete for, or win, the larger, national or international contracts, due to their limited resources, particularly for large local or regional contracts, BuildRight regularly finds itself competing against these same two companies.

In order to be able to respond to the market and fulfil their contracts to the required standards, on schedule and on budget, larger construction companies require a highly developed organisational framework or hierarchy, which makes clear management responsibilities and lines of communication between workers.

Figure 1 shows the company structure of Complex Construction Ltd.

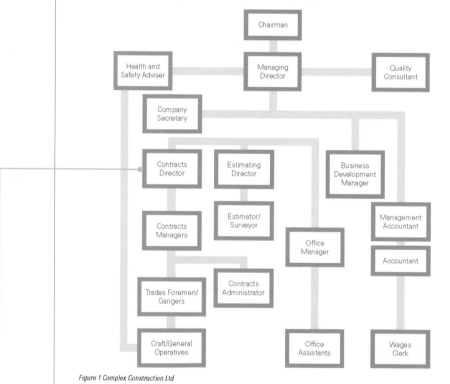

Figure 1 Complex Construction Ltd

Attention to detail in distinction level work is very important. In this chart the learner should have checked that the Contracts Director and Estimating Director should connect to the Managing Director.

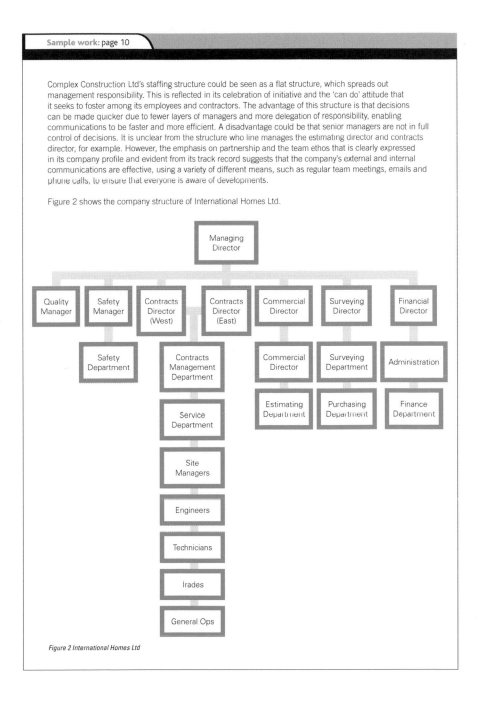

Sample work: page 10

Complex Construction Ltd's staffing structure could be seen as a flat structure, which spreads out management responsibility. This is reflected in its celebration of initiative and the 'can do' attitude that it seeks to foster among its employees and contractors. The advantage of this structure is that decisions can be made quicker due to fewer layers of managers and more delegation of responsibility, enabling communications to be faster and more efficient. A disadvantage could be that senior managers are not in full control of decisions. It is unclear from the structure who line manages the estimating director and contracts director, for example. However, the emphasis on partnership and the team ethos that is clearly expressed in its company profile and evident from its track record suggests that the company's external and internal communications are effective, using a variety of different means, such as regular team meetings, emails and phone calls, to ensure that everyone is aware of developments.

Figure 2 shows the company structure of International Homes Ltd.

Figure 2 International Homes Ltd

At distinction level you need to be clear, concise and to the point. This evaluation is too wordy and doesn't answer the question clearly enough.

There is some mention of lines of communication in the evaluation of the two companies, but there needs to be more evidence of this as it is clearly asked for in the task.

Sample work: page 11

International Homes Ltd's staffing structure could be seen as a top-down structure with clear lines of responsibility. An advantage of this type of structure is that the senior management team are always in control of decision-making; a disadvantage might be that decision-making could take a long time as questions need to be passed up the communication line to get an answer. The framework for this company is simpler to understand, however, with each employee having clear lines of communication and responsibility.

The person at the top of both structures is the sole person in charge of the business. This person has direct relationships vertically downwards. A lateral relationship is where many people have the same responsibility at the same level. Service or functional relationships are between people who work within a certain function. For example, a Contracts Director will be responsible for contracting-in work and is assisted by site managers and contracts managers. Your line manager will be the person you report to and the person who will give you instructions. Lateral relationships and modes of communication are evidently more relevant to the larger company structure of International Homes Ltd, as there are multiple managers at the same level in most of the departments.

The promotion of equality and diversity is extremely important within a construction company and will assist in providing an excellent working environment for all employees, in which they will respect and value one another. It is important that females are encouraged to enter the industry as they are under-represented and need to be given equal opportunities alongside male colleagues. Representatives of both companies' management team, together with managers representing BuildRight, regularly attend a regional Equal Opportunities and Diversity Group to consider best practice in all areas of business.

Staff development ensures that members of staff are well qualified to do what they do. International Homes Ltd's greater resources enable it to provide a greater measure of the necessary training in health and safety, asbestos awareness, manual handling, working at height, etc. in house. With only a single advisor on health and safety, and a quality consultant who is independent of the company, Complex Construction has fewer resources and must contract out most of its training and development requirements to external training providers.

Sample assessor's comment

This box will clearly illustrate whether you have met the grading criteria being assessed within this assignment.

Make sure that you leave feedback to the assessor. This helps you to think about how you have done and also helps the assessor decide if this method of assessment is working well, or needs to be changed.

Qualification	BTEC Level 2 Diploma in Construction	Year	2010–2011
Unit number and title	Unit 1: Structure of the Construction Industry	Learner name	Ryan Wilson

Grading criteria	Achieved?
P4 identify the personnel working in the construction industry	Yes
P5 describe the roles and responsibilities of the personnel working in the construction industry	Yes
P6 identify the qualifications, training and development needed to support careers in the construction industry	Yes
M3 explain how operatives and craftspersons can develop their careers and progress to a technical or professional role in a given area of activity	Yes
D2 evaluate two different organisational frameworks in terms of how they affect the interactions between members of the construction team	No

Learner feedback

I enjoyed doing the research for this assignment and learnt a lot from doing it. I didn't realise there was as many different job roles in the construction industry. I can see that I need to be more specific in my answers and really read and understand the question properly to achieve the distinction criterion. I also need to give evidence for every part of the task.

Assessor feedback

There are some really good aspects of this assignment Ryan. You have obviously done some very thorough research on the occupations within the construction industry. You need to do more work to be clearer in your analyses. Also make sure you pay really careful attention to detail when using technical terms.

Action plan

Try and practice your evaluation skills and make sure the companies you select to look at in assignments meet the needs for the criterion you're looking at. Keep an eye on the structure of your descriptions.

Assessor signature	D Jones	Date	14 November 2010
Learner signature	Ryan Wilson	Date	14 November 2010

The action plan is important and will be decided by you and your tutor. It will help you decide what you need to improve on in future assignments.

Coping with problems

Most learners sail through their BTEC First with no major problems. Unfortunately, not everyone is so lucky. Some may have personal difficulties or other issues that disrupt their work so they are late handing in their assignments. If this happens to you, it's vital to know what to do. This checklist should help.

Checklist for coping with problems

✔ Check that you know who to talk to.

✔ Don't sit on a problem and worry about it. Talk to someone promptly, in confidence. It's always easier to cope if you've shared it with someone.

✔ Most centres have professional counsellors you can talk to if you prefer. They won't repeat anything you say to them without your permission.

✔ If you've done something wrong or silly, people will respect you more if you are honest, admit where you went wrong and apologise promptly.

Case study: Getting help with personal problems

Initially, Rebecca made a good start on the BTEC First course and was really enjoying learning. Her dream is to become an architect and she was coping well with the assessments until recently. However, her parents have just split up and that is all she can think about – the upset is causing her studies to suffer.

Rebecca's college tutor senses that something is wrong with her concentration and sees that the standard of her work has declined. Not wanting to pry too deeply, he asks her if she would like to have a confidential, one-to-one chat with the college counsellor. Rebecca makes an appointment and goes along for a discussion.

Afterwards she feels a lot better. The counsellor helps her realise that she is having a normal reaction to a difficult period in her life, but that she will feel better in time. Counsellors are specialists in the type of problems young people experience and are perfectly qualified to help.

Rebecca appreciates the support that she is given and eventually comes to terms with her parents' separation. She manages to concentrate on her studies again, achieving three distinction grades in her first year. She looks back and reflects that she has learned a lot about herself in this period in her life.

TOP TIP

If you have a serious complaint or concern, talk to your chosen tutor first – for example if you believe an assignment grade is unfair. All centres have official procedures to cover important issues such as appeals about assignments and formal complaints. However, it's usually sensible to try to resolve a problem informally first.

Skills building

To do your best in your assignments you need a number of skills, including:

- your **personal, learning and thinking skills**
- your **functional skills** of ICT, mathematics and English
- your proofreading and document-production skills.

Personal, learning and thinking skills (PLTS)

These are the skills, personal qualities and behaviour that you find in people who are effective and confident at work. These people enjoy carrying out a wide range of tasks, always try to do their best and work well alone or with others. They enjoy a challenge and use new experiences to learn and develop.

Activity: How good are your PLTS?

1 Do this quiz to help you identify areas for improvement.

   a) I get on well with other people.

   Always   Usually   Seldom   Never

   b) I try to find out other people's suggestions for solving problems that puzzle me.

   Always   Usually   Seldom   Never

   c) I plan carefully to make sure I meet my deadlines.

   Always   Usually   Seldom   Never

   d) If someone is being difficult, I think carefully before making a response.

   Always   Usually   Seldom   Never

   e) I don't mind sharing my possessions or my time.

   Always   Usually   Seldom   Never

   f) I take account of other people's views and opinions.

   Always   Usually   Seldom   Never

   g) I enjoy thinking of new ways of doing things.

   Always   Usually   Seldom   Never

   h) I like creating new and different things.

   Always   Usually   Seldom   Never

   i) I enjoy planning and finding ways of solving problems.

   Always   Usually   Seldom   Never

j) I enjoy getting feedback about my performance.

Always   Usually   Seldom   Never

k) I try to learn from constructive criticism so that I know what to improve.

Always   Usually   Seldom   Never

l) I enjoy new challenges.

Always   Usually   Seldom   Never

m) I am even-tempered.

Always   Usually   Seldom   Never

n) I am happy to make changes when necessary.

Always   Usually   Seldom   Never

o) I like helping other people.

Always   Usually   Seldom   Never

Score 3 points for each time you answered 'Always', 2 points for 'Usually', 1 point for 'Seldom' and 0 points for 'Never'. The higher your score, the higher your personal, learning and thinking skills.

2   How creative are you? Test yourself with this activity. Identify 50 different objects you could fit into a matchbox at the same time! As a start, three suitable items are a postage stamp, a grain of rice, a staple. Can you find 47 more?

Functional skills

Functional skills are the practical skills you need to function confidently, effectively and independently at work, when studying and in everyday life. They focus on the following areas:

- Information and Communications Technology (ICT)
- Maths
- English.

You may already be familiar with functional skills. Your BTEC First tutors will give you more information about how you will continue to develop these skills on your new course.

ICT skills

These will relate directly to how much 'hands-on' practice you have had on IT equipment. You may be an experienced IT user and using word processing, spreadsheet and presentation software may be second nature. Searching for information online may be something you do every day – in between downloading music, buying or selling on eBay and updating your Facebook profile!

BTEC FACTS

Your BTEC First qualification is at Level 2. Qualifications in functional skills start at Entry level and continue to Level 2. (You don't need to achieve functional skills to gain any BTEC qualification and the evidence from a BTEC assignment can't be used towards the assessment of functional skills.)

Or you may prefer to avoid computer contact as much as possible. If so, there are two things you need to do.

1 Use every opportunity to improve your ICT skills so that you can start to live in the 21st century!

2 Make life easier by improving your basic proofreading and document preparation skills.

Proofreading and document preparation skills

Being able to produce well-displayed work quickly will make your life a lot easier. On any course there will be at least one unit that requires you to use good document preparation skills.

Tips to improve your document production skills

✔ If your keyboarding skills are poor, ask if there is a workshop you can join. Or your library or resource centre may have software you can use.

✔ Check that you know the format of documents you have to produce for assignments. It can help to have a 'model' version of each type in your folder for quick reference.

✔ Practise checking your work by reading word by word – and remember not to rely on spellcheckers.

Activity: How good are your ICT skills?

1a) Test your current ICT abilities by responding *honestly* to each of the following statements.

i) I can create a copy of my timetable using a word-processing or spreadsheet package.
True   **False**

ii) I can devise and design a budget for myself for the next three months using a spreadsheet package.
True   **False**

iii) I can email a friend who has just got broadband to say how to minimise the danger of computer viruses, what a podcast is and also explain the restrictions on music downloads.
True   **False**

iv) I can use presentation software to prepare a presentation containing four or five slides on a topic of my choice.
True   **False**

v) I can research online to compare the performance and prices of laptop computers and prepare an information sheet using word-processing software.
True   **False**

vi) I can prepare a poster, with graphics, for my mother's friend, who is starting her own business preparing children's party food, and attach it to an email to her for approval.
True   **False**

TRY THIS

Learning to touch type can save you hours of time. Go to page 98 to find out how to access a useful website where you can check your keyboarding skills.

TOP TIP

Print your work on good quality paper and keep it flat so that it looks good when you hand it in.

1b) Select any one of the above to which you answered false and learn how to do it.

2 Compare the two tables below. The first is an original document; the second is a typed copy. Are they identical? Highlight any differences you find and check them with the key on page 97.

Name	Date	Time	Room
Abbott	16 July	9.30 am	214
Grey	10 August	10.15 am	160
Johnston	12 August	2.20 pm	208
Waverley	18 July	3.15 pm	180
Jackson	30 September	11.15 am	209
Gregory	31 August	4.20 pm	320
Marshall	10 September	9.30 am	170
Bradley	16 September	2.20 pm	210

Name	Date	Time	Room
Abbott	26 July	9.30 am	214
Gray	10 August	10.15 am	160
Johnson	12 August	2.20 pm	208
Waverley	18 July	3.15 am	180
Jackson	31 September	11.15 am	209
Gregory	31 August	4.20 pm	320
Marshall	10 September	9.30 pm	170
Bradley	16 August	2.20 pm	201

Maths or numeracy skills

Four easy ways to improve your numeracy skills

1 Work out simple calculations in your head, like adding up the prices of items you are buying. Then check if you are correct when you pay for them.

2 Set yourself numeracy problems based on your everyday life. For example, if you are on a journey that takes 35 minutes and you leave home at 11.10am, what time will you arrive? If you are travelling at 40 miles an hour, how long will it take you to go 10 miles?

3 Treat yourself to a Maths Training program.

4 Check out online sites to improve your skills. Go to page 98 to find out how to access a useful website.

TOP TIP

Quickly test your answers. For example, if fuel costs 85p a litre and someone is buying 15 litres, estimate this at £1 x 15 (£15) and the answer should be just below this. So if your answer came out at £140, you'd know that immediately you'd done something wrong!

Activity: How good are your maths skills?

Answer as many of the following questions as you can in 15 minutes. Check your answers with the key on page 97.

1 a) 12 + 28 = ?

   i) 30   **ii) 34**   **iii) 38**   **iv) 40**   **v) 48**

b) 49 ÷ 7 = ?

   i) 6   **ii) 7**   **iii) 8**   **iv) 9**   **v) 10**

c) ½ + 1¼ = ?

   i) ¾   **ii) 1½**   **iii) 1¾**   **iv) 2¼**   **v) 3**

d) 4 × 12 = 8 × ?

   i) 5   **ii) 6**   **iii) 7**   **iv) 8**   **v) 9**

e) 16.5 + 25.25 – ? = 13.25

   i) 28.5   **ii) 31.25**   **iii) 34.5**   **iv) 41.65**   **v) 44**

2 a) You buy four items at £1.99, two at 98p and three at £1.75. You hand over a £20 note. How much change will you get? _____

b) What fraction of one litre is 250 ml? _____

c) What percentage of £50 is £2.50? _____

d) A designer travelling on business can claim 38.2p a mile in expenses. How much is she owed if she travels 625 miles? _____

e) You are flying to New York in December. New York is five hours behind British time and the flight lasts eight hours. If you leave at 11.15 am, what time will you arrive? _____

f) For your trip to the United States you need American dollars. You find that the exchange rate is $1.5 dollars.

   i) How many dollars will you receive if you exchange £500? _____

   ii) Last year your friend visited New York when the exchange rate was $1.8. She also exchanged £500. Did she receive more dollars than you or fewer – and by how much? _____

g) A security guard and his dog patrol the perimeter fence of a warehouse each evening. The building is 480 metres long and 300 metres wide and the fence is 80 metres out from the building on all sides. If the guard and his dog patrol the fence three times a night, how far will they walk? _____

English skills

Your English skills affect your ability to understand what you read, prepare a written document, say what you mean and understand other people. Even if you're doing a practical subject, there will always be times when you need to leave someone a note, tell them about a phone call, read or listen to instructions – or write a letter for a job application!

Six easy ways to improve your English skills

1 Read more. It increases the number of words you know and helps to make you familiar with correct spellings.

2 Look up words you don't understand in a dictionary and check their meaning. Then try to use them yourself to increase your vocabulary.

3 Do crosswords. These help increase your vocabulary and practise your spelling at the same time.

4 You can use websites to help you get to grips with English vocabulary, grammar and punctuation. Go to page 98 to find out how to access a useful website for this page.

5 Welcome opportunities to practise speaking in class, in discussion groups and during presentations – rather than avoiding them!

6 Test your ability to listen to someone else by seeing how much you can remember when they've finished speaking.

Activity: How good are your English skills?

1 In the table below are 'wrong' versions of words often spelled incorrectly. Write the correct spellings on the right. Check your list against the answers on page 97.

Incorrect spelling	Correct spelling
accomodation	
seperate	
definate	
payed	
desparate	
acceptible	
competant	
succesful	

2 Correct the error(s) in these sentences.

   a) The plug on the computer is lose.

   b) The car was stationery outside the house.

   c) Their going on they're holidays tomorrow.

   d) The principle of the college is John Smith.

   e) We are all going accept Tom.

3 Punctuate these sentences correctly.

   a) Toms train was late on Monday and Tuesday.

   b) She is going to France Belgium Spain and Italy in the summer.

   c) He comes from Leeds and says its great there.

4 Read the article on copyright.

Copyright

Anyone who uses a photocopier can break copyright law if they carry out unrestricted photocopying of certain documents. This is because The Copyright, Designs and Patents Act 1988 protects the creator of an original work against having it copied without permission.

Legally, every time anyone writes a book, composes a song, makes a film or creates any other type of artistic work, this work is treated as their property (or copyright). If anyone else wishes to make use of it, they must get permission to do so and, on occasions, pay a fee.

Licences can be obtained to allow educational establishments to photocopy limited numbers of some publications. In addition, copies of an original document can be made for certain specific purposes. These include research and private study. Under the Act, too, if an article is summarised and quoted by anyone, then the author and title of the original work must be acknowledged.

a) Test your ability to understand unfamiliar information by responding to the following statements with 'True' or 'False'.

   i) Students and tutors in schools and colleges can copy anything they want.
   True   False

   ii) The law which covers copyright is The Copyright, Designs and Patents Act 1988.
   True   False

   iii) A student photocopying a document in the library must have a licence.
   True   False

   iv) Copyright only relates to books in the library.
   True   False

   v) If you quote a newspaper report in an assignment, you don't need to state the source.
   True   False

   vii) Anyone is allowed to photocopy a page of a book for research purposes.
   True   False

b) Make a list of key points in the article, then write a brief summary in your own words.

5 Nikki has read a newspaper report that a horse racing in the Kentucky Derby had to be put down. The filly collapsed and the vet couldn't save her. Nikki says it's the third time in two years a racehorse has had to be put down in the US. As a horse lover she is convinced racing should be banned in Britain and the US. She argues that fox hunting was banned to protect foxes, and that racehorses are more important and more expensive than foxes. Darren disagrees. He says the law is not working, hardly anyone has been prosecuted and fox hunting is going on just like before. Debbie says that animals aren't important whilst there is famine in the world.

a) Do you think the three arguments are logical? See if you can spot the flaws and check your ideas with the suggestions on page 97.

b) Sporting activities and support for sporting teams often provoke strong opinions. For a sport or team of your choice, identify two opposing views that might be held. Then decide how you would give a balanced view. Test your ideas with a friend or family member.

Answers

Skills building answers

ICT activities

2 Differences between the two tables are highlighted in bold.

Name	Date	Time	Room
Abbott	**16** July	9.30 am	214
Grey	10 August	10.15 am	160
Johnston	12 August	2.20 pm	208
Waverley	18 July	3.15 **pm**	180
Jackson	**30** September	11.15 am	209
Gregory	31 August	4.20 pm	320
Marshall	10 September	9.30 **am**	170
Bradley	16 **September**	2.20 pm	**210**

Maths/numeracy activities

1 **a)** iv, **b)** ii, **c)** iii, **d)** ii, **e)** i

2 **a)** £4.83, **b)** ¼, **c)** 5%, **d)** £238.75, **e)** 2.15 pm, **f) i)** $750 **ii)** $150 dollars more, **g)** 6.6 km.

English activities

1 Spellings: accommodation, separate, definite, paid, desperate, acceptable, competent, successful

2 Errors:
a) The plug on the computer is <u>loose</u>.
b) The car was <u>stationary</u> outside the house.
c) <u>They're</u> going on <u>their</u> holidays tomorrow.
d) The <u>principal</u> of the college is John Smith.
e) We are all going <u>except</u> Tom.

3 Punctuation:
a) Tom's train was late on Monday and Tuesday.
b) She is going to France, Belgium, Spain and Italy in the summer.
c) He comes from Leeds and says it's great there.

4 **a) i)** False, **ii)** True, **iii)** False, **iv)** False, **v)** False, **vi)** False, **vii)** True

5 A logical argument would be that if racehorses are frequently injured in a particular race, eg one with difficult jumps, then it should not be held. It is not logical to compare racehorses with foxes. The value of the animal is irrelevant if you are assessing cruelty. Darren's argument is entirely different and unrelated to Nikki's. Whether or not fox hunting legislation is effective or not has no bearing on the danger (or otherwise) to racehorses. Finally, famine is a separate issue altogether. You cannot logically 'rank' problems in the world to find a top one and ignore the others until this is solved!

Accessing website links

Links to various websites are referred to throughout this BTEC Level 2 First Study Skills Guide. In order to ensure that these links are up-to-date, that they work and that the sites aren't inadvertently linked to any material that could be considered offensive, we have made the links available on our website: www.pearsonhotlinks.co.uk. When you visit the site, search for either the title BTEC Level 2 First Study Skills Guide in Construction or ISBN 9781846905766. From here you can gain access to the website links and information on how they can be used to help you with your studies.

Useful terms

Apprenticeships
Schemes that enable you to work and earn money at the same time as you gain further qualifications (an NVQ award and a technical certificate) and improve your functional skills. Apprentices learn work-based skills relevant to their job role and their chosen industry. See page 98 for how to access a useful website to find out more.

Assessment methods
Methods, such as practical tasks and assignments, which are used to check that your work demonstrates the learning and understanding you need to obtain the qualification.

Assessor
The tutor who marks or assesses your work.

Assignment
A complete task or mini-**project** set to meet specific grading criteria.

Assignment brief
The information and instructions related to a particular assignment.

BTEC Level 3 Nationals
Qualifications you can take when you have successfully achieved a Level 2 qualification, such as BTEC First. BTEC Level 3 Nationals are offered in a variety of subjects.

Credit value
The number of credits attached to your BTEC course. The credit value increases relative to the length of time you need to complete the course, from 15 credits for a BTEC Certificate, to 30 credits for a BTEC Extended Certificate and 60 credits for a BTEC Diploma.

Command word
The word in an assignment that tells you what you have to do to produce the type of answer that is required, eg 'list', 'describe', 'analyse'.

Educational Maintenance Award (EMA)
This is a means-tested award which provides eligible learners under 19, who are studying a full-time course at a centre, with a cash sum of money every week. See page 98 for how to access a useful website to find out more.

Functional skills
The practical skills that enable all learners to use and apply English, Maths and ICT both at work and in their everyday lives. They aren't compulsory to achieve on the course, but are of great use to you.

Grade
The rating of pass, merit or distinction that is given to an assignment you have completed, which identifies the standard you have achieved.

Grading criteria
The standard you have to demonstrate to obtain a particular grade in the unit. In other words, what you have to prove you can do.

Grading grid
The table in each unit of your BTEC qualification specification that sets out the grading criteria.

Indicative reading
Recommended books, magazines, journals and websites whose content is both suitable and relevant to the unit.

Induction
A short programme of events at the start of a course or work placement designed to give you essential information and introduce you to other people so that you can settle in easily.

Internal verification
The quality checks carried out by nominated tutors at all centres to ensure that all assignments are at the right level and cover appropriate learning outcomes. The checks also ensure that all **assessors** are marking work consistently and to the same standards.

Learning outcomes
The learning and skills you must demonstrate to show that you have learned a unit effectively.

Levels of study

The depth, breadth and complexity of knowledge, understanding and skills required to achieve a qualification determines its level. Level 2 is equivalent to GCSE level (grades A* to C). Level 3 equates to GCE A-level. As you successfully achieve one level, you can progress on to the next. BTEC qualifications are offered at Entry Level, then Levels 1, 2, 3, 4, 5, 6 and 7.

Mandatory units

On a BTEC Level 2 First course, these are the compulsory units that all learners must complete to gain the qualification.

Optional units

Units on your course from which you may be able to make a choice. They help you specialise your skills, knowledge and understanding and may help progression into work or further education.

Personal, learning and thinking skills (PLTS)

The skills and qualities that improve your ability to work independently and be more effective and confident at work. Opportunities for developing these are a feature of all BTEC First courses. They aren't compulsory to achieve on the course, but are of great use to you.

Plagiarism

Copying someone else's work or work from any other sources (eg the internet) and passing it off as your own. It is strictly forbidden on all courses.

Portfolio

A collection of work compiled by a learner – for an **assessor** – usually as evidence of learning.

Project

A comprehensive piece of work which normally involves original research and planning and investigation either by an individual or a team. The outcome will vary depending upon the type of project undertaken. For example, it may result in the organisation of a specific event, a demonstration of a skill, a presentation or a piece of writing.

Tutorial

An individual or small group meeting with your tutor at which you discuss the work you are currently doing and other more general course issues.

Unit content

Details about the topics covered by the unit and the knowledge and skills you need to complete it.

Work placement

Time spent on an employer's premises when you carry out work-based tasks as an employee and also learn about the enterprise to develop your skills and knowledge.

Work-related qualification

A qualification designed to help you to develop the knowledge and understanding you need for a particular area of work.